still
life

A MEMOIR

Jeff Sutherland, M.D.

sh.
SUTHERLAND
HOUSE

TORONTO, 2019

Sutherland House
416 Moore Ave., Suite 205
Toronto, ON M4G 1C9

Sutherland House and logo are registered
trademarks of The Sutherland House Inc.

First hardcover edition, September 2019

If you are interested in inviting one of our authors to a live event or
media appearance, please contact publicity@sutherlandhousebooks.com
and visit our website at sutherlandhousebooks.com for more
information about our authors and their schedules.

Manufactured in Canada
Cover designed by Lena Yang
Book composed by Karl Hunt

Library and Archives Canada Cataloguing in Publication
Title: Still life : a memoir / Jeff Sutherland.
Names: Sutherland, Jeff, 1966- author.
Identifiers: Canadiana 2019013223X | ISBN 9781999439569 (hardcover)
Subjects: LCSH: Sutherland, Jeff, 1966- | LCSH: Amyotrophic
lateral sclerosis—Patients—Canada—Biography. |
LCSH: Amyotrophic lateral sclerosis—Patients—
Family relationships—Canada. | LCGFT: Autobiographies.
Classification: LCC RC406.A24 S88 2019 |
DDC 362.1968/390092—dc23

ISBN 978-1-9994395-6-9

EDITOR'S NOTE

I F A DEBILITATING AND terminal illness had been all that befell Dr. Jeff Sutherland, his story would still be remarkable. Having lost the use his limbs and all of his voluntary muscles, and along with those his flourishing career as a family physician, having lost the ability to speak, to swallow, to breathe without an external apparatus, he found the courage to accept and adapt to his condition and forge a meaningful new life for himself. With determination, technological assistance, and the support of his family, he was able to remain a vital presence in their lives and continue his involvement in his community, contributing to an extent that many able-bodied people cannot match. But Jeff Sutherland's battle with ALS is just the overture to this unconventional memoir.

It diminishes neither the magnitude of his loss or the fortitude he displayed to note that he had certain advantages in fighting his illness. He was intelligent, physically fit, and in the prime of life at age forty-one. He was a medical doctor, a man of action, one of life's high achievers, with an abundance of resources to see him through, not least of these a loving family, a wide circle of friends, and a certain confidence and resilience reinforced by the full and happy life he had lived until illness struck. He made the most of his time before his disease had done its worst and he prepared himself as best he could for the inanimate state awaiting him. He was not so well positioned when greater tragedy struck.

A man who in his darker moments believed himself to have lost everything was staggered to find that he could, and would, lose far more. Nothing in life can prepare a person for the death of a child. That it happened in a sudden, freak accident made it all the more shocking, and senseless, and difficult to endure. The loss of Jeff Sutherland's twenty-one-year-old son, Zachary, and his girlfriend Kaya, is where this story truly begins. It dropped his father into an abyss that his own disease had never plumbed, shattering his soul and bringing him to the realization that even with ALS, he had lived a relatively unexamined life. It left him questioning his religious beliefs, the nature of the human spirit, the meaning of death, his scientific worldview, his closest relationships, his desire to go on living. He had no analogues for what he was feeling and no vocabulary to express his confusion and pain. His journey back from this abyss is the heart of his story.

It was not an easy journey, nor a quick one. It was complicated by his physical condition, and it will never be finished. It involved a long and wrenching struggle with grief, an excruciating amount of searching and personal growth, and a complete reconsideration of his core values. It raised the most profound questions a person can ask: is survival always worth the struggle, and how does one find meaning in the face of cruel tragedy? It was the hardest work of Dr. Sutherland's life, undertaken in the stillness of his physical state, accomplished in his heart and mind and recorded on a computer screen mounted eighteen inches in front of his face and manipulated by his eyes, the only parts of his body he can still control. A characteristically reticent man, he related his entire experience with stunning candor, holding back none of the depression, guilt, and despair he felt along the way, nor the love that, more than anything, allowed him to heal and gradually, tentatively reclaim the sense of purpose and even the joy he had known in his former life.

Still Life will challenge what you believe about loss, tragedy, death, and grief, and make you think about where and how you find meaning in life. At the same time, it is as uplifting a book as you will ever read. For all he has suffered, Dr. Sutherland is grateful for being alive, whatever his limitations, and convinced that the human spirit can triumph over any tragedy, and that a good life is within reach of every person no matter how extreme his or her circumstances. He distills his experience into sage advice on how to persevere and flourish in the face of adversity, whether health troubles, relationship problems, job loss, or the death of a loved one, and how to help others do the same.

It was no easy feat for Dr. Sutherland to give the world what he acknowledges is "a brutally frank" look at his life but because he has done so, no one who reads his book will ever need to face adversity without hope, or to feel that he or she is doing so alone.

Kenneth Whyte, Sutherland House, 2019

CONTENTS

Loss and Change

CHANGE IS AN INEVITABLE part of life. Sometimes we initiate it, sometimes it comes to us suddenly on its own terms, and sometimes it can be slow and insidious, apparent only in retrospect. This book deals with all kinds of change but it focuses on that which we would prefer to avoid: change that occurs against our will. That everyone faces this type of challenge at some point in life is no consolation when we are embroiled in it. No one wants these changes and still they come. When a negative change occurs, we have to choose how we will face it. We can be paralyzed with fear or we can adapt to our new reality. We can make the choice to integrate it into our life, make peace with it, and eventually grow from it. With any change, good or bad, personal growth is the ideal outcome. It is my belief that this is part of our soul's mission on earth.

In this book, I will often speak of loss. We have all suffered loss, or we will in time, either ourselves or through someone we love, despite living in a society that minimizes loss as though it is a rarity. Deep personal loss for some unknown reason has wrapped its tentacles around my family and me for the last twelve years of my life. My losses have at certain points felt unbearable, and still I lost more. I will tell this story with the only tool I have left for communication:

my eyes. It is a story about living with extreme limitations and trying to make peace with and still prosper with what the universe has
given my family and me, both good and bad. It is about love and
the efforts we have made to integrate our losses into our lives in
a healing manner. With the tragedies we have had to endure, the
greatest would be if we enabled more tragedy to ripple throughout
our future lives.

If you are reading this, you may have suffered a serious loss in
your life. The type of loss that shakes you to your core and makes
you question your continued existence. Or you may not yet have
faced loss and are reading with a sense of dread about the inevitable,
wondering if you will be able to endure it when it comes. During
times of seemingly unending darkness, you may wonder if other
people who have faced profound loss eventually find peace and happiness again. The simple answer is yes, it is possible, but it takes a
lot of work. It requires you to challenge your belief systems and
summon your deepest reserves of will. Throughout the process of
healing, you will need love. Some days you will not feel loved, or find
the ability to love others. You will feel very much alone. This is the
path of grief after any loss. It can be very solitary but with the support of loved ones you will find purpose and meaning in your life,
and by giving love to others and to yourself, you will find the path
to happiness. Through the active work of reading, reflection, and
mindfulness you can eventually find some peace in your situation.

When negative change enters your life, you have to decide for
yourself the whys of fighting for some level of peace. The whys for
me have always been my loving wife and my three sons. They have
always been my priority, especially following my tragedies. To successfully fight you have to find your why. Once it is found, the how
will follow.

Self and spirituality are prominent in this book. Spirituality can
be a specific religious devotion but I prefer a more inclusive path.

Whether you call the divine presence God, Allah, Buddha, Source, or any other name from another religious or even nonreligious tradition does not matter in the end. What matters is the recognition that we are all interconnected with everything that is and was, through love.

CHAPTER ONE

"I Have What?"

I N THE FALL OF 2007, I knew something was off and when I think back and connect the dots there were hints even before. During the previous hockey season, especially when digging in the corners of the rink, I noticed I was losing forearm strength. Then my left arm started losing strength when I was doing dumbbell curls at the gym. My muscle twitching started about six months later. These changes occurred about a year before my diagnosis. Stress, coffee, and a pinched nerve from an old soccer injury, I told myself but deep down, having graduated from medical school and practiced for more than a decade, I knew it was amyotrophic lateral sclerosis, familiarly known as ALS, or Lou Gehrig's disease, and I knew that there was nothing I could do about it. By late October 2007, I decided to see a specialist.

"My darn left arm keeps twitching," I said to the neurologist. After taking a brief history of my health and giving me a physical exam, he started poking tiny needles into my arms and legs. He conducted the electromyography (EMG) testing that we both knew I needed. After the tests, he brought me into a shabby, dimly lit office and said hesitantly, "There is a ninety percent chance you have ALS." Just like that, the worries I had kept hidden from everyone else during the previous year were confirmed.

Until that moment, my life had been fantastic. I knew it was fantastic and I was thankful for all the gifts I had been given, and that my family had been given. I was forty-one. My professional life was flourishing. I had a very busy and rewarding hospital practice delivering babies, and working in both the emergency department and on the hospital wards. I was teaching the art of medicine to family-medicine residents and was helping with the administration of the hospital system. I also had a very busy and rewarding office practice. It was not a job for me but a calling.

On the personal side, I had a love affair with my wife, Darlene, that was only growing stronger with time. We had a nice routine of working out together and grabbing a coffee afterward, and Darlene had started a promising small business with our sister-in-law. Our three sons, Zach, Ben, and Nathaniel were happy and healthy and I was involved in their activities. I was volunteering: as a coach in numerous sports, in a service club, and as a chalice bearer at church. On my fortieth birthday, I had made hot dogs at the opening day for our youth soccer club with the Kinsmen while Darlene was picking up our first "toy," a black BMW convertible.

In addition to thinking—knowing—that I had a great life, I had considered myself to be in excellent physical shape, although that turned out to be an illusion, given that I had an eighty percent probability of dying in the next five years. I took the devastating news and returned to the confines of my bright blue-and-white office, knowing that I had to tell Darlene about my diagnosis and that in a few years I would change from the person she knew to someone who was unable to move or speak. She had known about my symptoms but we had never discussed the possibility that ALS could be the reason for them. I picked up the telephone.

"I need to tell you something," I said quietly and calmly. "I have seen the neurologist. He thinks I have ALS."

Darlene responded with questions that could not be answered then or, for that matter, now. "What? How? Why?"

"I'll be home early today, and we can talk about it more, honey."

I said that through tears, knowing I had broken the news unfairly and like a coward by using the telephone, but knowing I had to tell her and put the shock of the diagnosis behind me and strive for normality. I finished my sandwich and saw my first patient of the afternoon. I wanted to hear my patients' problems to get my mind off my own problem. I did cancel my last hour at the clinic, though, and raced home to see what damage I had inflicted on my family.

As I came into the house, Zach hollered, "Hey Dad, remember we have a practice tonight." I found Darlene upstairs. She had stayed in bed most of the afternoon and called a friend to help console her. I took off my loafers, closed the door, and climbed into bed beside her. We hugged and cried and talked about what to tell the boys.

That evening, we called a meeting around the kitchen island. Nathaniel, age ten, wondered what he or his brothers could have done so wrong that a meeting was required. Some people do not discuss serious health problems with their children right away and that is a personal decision. For us, we felt that the diagnosis was certain and we did not want to keep such an important issue secret. We knew the boys would be able to see the changes in our behavior. Worse still would be if they heard about it accidentally from someone other than us.

"We need to tell you something important," I began. "I have this disease that with time will make me weaker and weaker. We don't know how quickly this will occur and since I am only forty-one, I will do better than most."

"Dad, will you be able to golf with me next year?" Zach, age thirteen, asked.

"Yes, and unfortunately you will still be able to beat me by twenty strokes."

Ben, eleven, was numb with shock and did not know what to think or what questions to ask. When I think back to that moment, we were all numb and in shock. Ben reflected how we were all feeling.

We kept things as positive as we could, not knowing if the illness would progress slowly or quickly. We told the boys that the choice was between living with the disease and dying with the disease, and we were choosing to live with it, and we wanted them on the journey with us. This would be the start of our new lives.

* * *

Maybe it was a coincidence, maybe it was foreshadowing, but ALS had been in my awareness from a young age. I remember when I was about eight years old watching a Saturday-afternoon movie called *The Pride of the Yankees* on our family's black-and-white television. It was about the life of Lou Gehrig, an outstanding baseball player in the 1920s and '30s who at the age of thirty-five was stricken with an illness that suddenly sapped his strength. The man they called the "Iron Horse" for his record of playing in 2,130 consecutive games finally asked to be taken out of the lineup because of his weakness. He felt he was hurting his team, and soon after he retired. On July 4, 1939, he gave his famous "I am the luckiest man on the face of the earth" speech to a sold-out crowd at Yankee Stadium. He passed away two years later. The movie and the illness known as Lou Gehrig's disease imprinted themselves on my young brain.

In medical school, I learned of the disease by its actual name, amyotrophic lateral sclerosis. Its nomenclature describes the pathology or damage that is seen upon autopsy in the spinal cords of people who die from the disease. It is incurable and it renders its victims totally paralyzed until they die, either because they are unable to eat or unable to breathe.

With an incidence of only 2.5 people in 100,000, ALS is a rare disease yet I have had a surprising amount of contact with it. During my medical training, a neighbor who was in his sixties was diagnosed with ALS. He died about two years after the diagnosis. During the early years of my practice, I was asked to see my sister-in-law's brother who had been having difficulty getting answers to why he could not stand easily from a seated position. I knew that his problems were neurological and referred him to a neurologist who subsequently diagnosed him with ALS. This man was in his early thirties. He was single and he had just started a career as a chef. As his symptoms got worse, he had to live with his parents. They cared for him lovingly and tirelessly and he lived until his late thirties, a tragic end to a life that had barely begun. About five years into my practice, I started caring for a man in his late sixties who had ALS. On my first house call, I saw a photograph of him taken a few years before his diagnosis. He was a powerful, muscular man. Eventually, his elderly wife was unable to meet the demands of looking after him and he was admitted to a long-term care center.

Probably the easiest way to describe what happens to a person with ALS is to say that the disease kills the nerves connected to all the muscles that we can consciously move. Because a victim is unable to move his or her muscles, they wither. First goes the strength, then all control. Voluntary muscles are not only those that permit us to walk and talk. They are also those that allow us to swallow and breathe. ALS does not impair a person's sight, hearing, or senses of taste, smell, or touch. Nor does it affect a person's bladder, bowel, or sexual function, and only occasionally does it affect the ability to move one's eyes or blink.

The illness usually presents first as stiffness, twitching muscles, muscle weakness and/or a hoarse voice. It can be difficult to diagnose in its early stages—there are many causes of stiffness, twitching, weakness and hoarseness. Eventually, it can be confirmed through electromyography (EMG), clinical exam, and by ruling out other diseases through blood tests, spinal fluid analysis, and magnetic resonance imaging (MRI) of the brain and neck (all of these tests would be done to me in the months following my initial consultation). For years, people thought it did not affect cognition in the brain but now researchers know that half of people with ALS have frontal lobe problems. These might manifest as mild changes in personality—becoming more opinionated, obstinate, and lacking in empathy. They might affect control of one's emotions, leading to inappropriate outbursts. Some victims have trouble remembering the names of people and common objects, while still others suffer profound frontal lobe dementia.

Not only is ALS incurable but there is really no effective treatment for it. Rilutek is the medication most commonly prescribed but trials show only that it delays the requirement for invasive ventilator support (tracheostomy) by about three months. Despite this small effect, Rilutek is commonly used by ALS patients when they can afford the $550 a month cost. A new drug, edaravone, was released in 2018. It has been shown to slow early ALS progression but how it helps long term has yet to be demonstrated. Scientists doubt there will ever be a single cure for ALS but hope to come up with a cocktail of treatments that will reduce it to a chronic illness, much as has been done for HIV. Research into the genetic causes of ALS and stem cell therapy may also someday help to slow its progress.

Little is known about the causes of ALS. In about five to ten percent of cases, it is inherited, passed directly from generation to generation through genetic mutations. The remaining cases, such as mine, are known as sporadic ALS. Although the environmental risk factors that contribute to a person developing ALS remain unknown there is a noticeably increased incidence in people who participate in sports in which there is repetitive head concussive trauma and cervical spinal trauma. This is particularly seen in professional soccer and football players. Other less quantifiable environmental risks include exposure to mercury, lead, solvents, and pesticides; military service; physically strenuous occupations; smoking; being electrically shocked; and viral infections. Otherwise, ALS does not discriminate. There is a roughly equal distribution of the disease by gender (although males have a slightly higher preponderance) and it affects all races. It has a peak in incidence at age fifty-eight to sixty but, as I have experienced, it can also present in young adults. Eighty percent of people with ALS die within three to five years of their diagnosis and only ten percent are alive ten years after. Living with the disease for more than fifty years, as Stephen Hawking did, is extremely rare.

This was the disease with which I was diagnosed at my neurological referral that day in October 2007.

CHAPTER TWO

A Fortunate Life

MY FAMILY IS FROM New Brunswick, a province where fishing, farming, lumber, oil refineries, and paper mills drive the local economies. A lot of my ancestors made their livelihoods in these industries but my grandparents on both sides ensured that their children had post–secondary educations. My father obtained his master's in civil engineering and my mother has a degree in nursing. They met in a small university town, fell in love, married, and had three sons—I landed in the middle—and after several moves we settled in Halifax, Nova Scotia, in a community of mostly young people who, like my parents, were first-generation professionals.

I was blessed with loving parents, although they did not regularly convey their emotions to their children as is common now. As kids, we enjoyed a freedom of movement that is unusual today. The world was a place to be explored, not feared. At age four, we had the run of our little street. By nine, we had the run of our subdivision. By eleven, we had the run of our part of town, through the transit system. My closest friends lived within a few houses of me and we would call on each other and play street hockey or hide-and-seek. I was not particularly close to my older brother, Brad, who was more than three years older than me and often away for the summer during our formative years. Later, we would bond while raising our young families. I was closer to Brent, only fifteen months behind me. We grew up together and shared a bedroom as well as organized activities—Scouts, hockey, football.

I was disappointed in junior high school not to be in the new advanced class that was offered in our school. It was filled with students judged to be gifted by the IQ measurements used in the mid-1970s. I knew a lot of the kids and I was frankly surprised that I had not made the cut. In high school, I excelled in most subjects, especially the sciences. I took a lot of honors courses, probably to compensate for not having been designated "gifted" in junior high school. I also took up football along with a friend. By senior year, I was our starting tailback, just 155 pounds and five foot eight but I could bench-press the full stack of 270 pounds on our universal weight machine. I took most of the handoffs behind my brother Brent on the offensive line. More of a grinder than a finesse running back, I remember being bruised and contused a lot that fall. We won some big games and after one important victory I was interviewed by the local newspaper while walking out of the stadium with my dad—I think he was proud of me in that moment. The season ended with a loss in the semifinals but three of us were named to the provincial all-star team and I received the team MVP award.

I mention these things from my school days not to boast or because I expect readers will find them particularly interesting but because those times seem worlds away from me now. I suppose every middle-aged person feels removed from his or her youth but I am a profoundly different person today. The idea of throwing a ball or lifting weights is beyond comprehension when you no longer have the requisite strength to compete with the forces of gravity. Much of what I once took for granted seems exotic in retrospect, although it would not be accurate to say that I am wholly disconnected from that boy. For one thing, he chose for me my true love and life's companion.

Before every dance in our senior year, my friends and I had a tradition of drinking behind a newspaper storage box on the way to our high school. On one of these nights, a Saturday in early April, one of my friends insisted on tequila shots. A couple of us feel for the promise of a good cheap drunk and contributed to the bottle but none of us took well to the tequila. "Lick the salt, drink the shot, suck on the orange slice," we were instructed. We added a fourth step of vomiting after each shot, yet persisted, thinking that we could get used to anything. We must have gotten a buzz from the bottle but I can still recall the events of that evening. In particular, I remember saying as we were walking to the dance, "I need to find a girlfriend."

We arrived at the school at nine thirty, by which time my younger brother had ended his night by passing his bottle of alcohol to our principal, mistaking him for a friend in an unlit space. I had just entered the gym when a friend said, "Hey Jeff, I have someone for you to meet." I still do not know why he introduced us but standing before me was an attractive girl I knew only by name. The disc jockey was playing Phil Collins's "Against All Odds" and we started dancing. It didn't take long before we started kissing, both of us being under the influence, and we kept on kissing for the next forty-five minutes.

We were a bit embarrassed by the kissing marathon that started our relationship and did not know what to do next. Three days passed and our paths did not cross. A few more days passed. On the Thursday, Darlene came to my locker and asked if I would like to come to her house for lunch on Friday. She lived close to the school. I readily accepted. On Friday, Darlene welcomed me into her modest home. We were alone because both of her parents worked. We kissed a little more and talked and made plans to go to a movie downtown, near where she worked part-time at a perfume boutique.

I got myself ready for the movie, met her at her work, and was surprised to find her alone in the boutique. The responsibility of closing and depositing the till was more than I would have expected for a grade twelve student. She did everything by the book and at nine we made our way to the Paramount Theatre on Barrington Street. On our way, we held hands and she started rubbing her thumb against mine, a little gesture of comfort on her part and a big turn-on for me. After the movie, we sat in Sir Sandford Fleming Park, known as "the Dingle" to Haligonians. On a clear night, the moonlight reflects on the shimmering water of the Northwest Arm, providing one of the most romantic views in town. We kissed some more and as if reliving a scene from *Happy Days*, I asked my first and last girlfriend to go steady with me.

* * *

My first big choice in life was made just after graduation. I had to decide if I would go away to university and play football or stay in Halifax, attend a university without a football program, and concentrate on academics with the goal of gaining admission to medical school. I chose the academic route and started at Dalhousie that fall. Darlene attended, too, although by the middle of our first winter, she had decided to become a clinical dietitian and to accomplish this she needed to transfer to another university in second year. The first in her family to attend university, Darlene was focused and determined to do well. She spent most weekends at her desk studying. I usually studied with her until around nine p.m. when we would put the books away and watch whatever movies we had rented. I was not seeing as much of the guys. I believe having Darlene to ground me on most weekends led to my success later in life.

I did well in my first year of university which boosted my hopes of becoming a physician, as did my score in MCAT testing. I applied to medical school during third year and when it came time for the interview, I was so nervous I locked my keys in the car. Fortunately, I recognized one of the interviewers as the father of a football teammate, which helped me relax, and by February, 1987, after a thorough review of my application, I was accepted into the program. Around the same time, I landed a summer job as the coordinator of Dalhousie University's summer orientation program. As coordinator of the program, I became comfortable with giving public addresses and leading the team which, while exhausting for an introvert like me, helped me develop confidence and leadership skills. I owe much to that job.

In the fall of 1987, I started my medical education at Dalhousie. There were a hundred students in our class, including some good friends from undergrad. It was a fantastic class, full of people who cared about one another and cooperated for everyone's success. From the lab work to the note-taking, we worked better together than alone. We spent much of our first and second years in two large lecture halls and in the micro-anatomy and gross-anatomy laboratories. In addition to forty hours a week of classes and labs, we spent another twenty hours a week individually assimilating what we had learned. On our lunch breaks, we built hockey nets out of pine boards and chicken wire and played street hockey in the courtyard. It became well organized, with teams and a schedule.

Initially, the most challenging part of my medical education was when we started to work with cadavers. It was humbling to think somebody had given their body to help with my education, and we were all hesitant to work with actual human parts. We were in groups of four, taking turns on the dissections. During first year, the heads of our cadavers were always wrapped. The dissection of the head and eventually the brain was a second-year endeavor. While at first I had found it humbling to think that somebody had given their body to help with my education, as the months progressed,

I believe they became mere bodies to us and I lost, as we all did, that sense of the preciousness of their gift. Looking back now, I know I should have kept the sanctity of their gift on my mind continuously but I did not. Something happens in medical education where you stop recognizing your patient as a person and instead see a diagnosis or a body. This is probably a defense mechanism that keeps us at a psychological distance from stressful events. Some of us find our way back to recognition of the importance of the person but some of us do not. This is a problem I have become especially sensitive to in my current state, and it is one the medical profession needs to work on.

Between my third and fourth years, a friend and I did a six-week elective at Black River in rural Jamaica, making hospital rounds, running clinics, assisting in surgeries. We were on call for emergencies and we delivered babies with midwives. We were practicing medicine in challenging and constrained circumstances, relying on our intuition as much as our skill. Jamaica was where I saw maggots used to debride wounds, where I first saw someone die on the operating table (in this case, after being stabbed in the chest), and where I saw deformed children abandoned by their families to state institutions. These months were the greatest educational opportunity I ever had, and through these Jamaican experiences I became a doctor. I accepted full responsibility for anyone that I had in my care.

After my Jamaica experience, my final-year clerkship, in which I was stuck in a subordinate position with no real responsibility, was a disappointment. In fact, the first-world medicine I learned in my last year of medical school, and all the politics that went with it, wore on me. I began to see Halifax as a specialist-centric environment, with not a lot of respect for family physicians, and I looked forward to leaving for a place where I could learn more than I would within its tertiary-care confines. I wanted to be a family physician despite most of my close friends opting for specialization. During my clinical rotations in smaller communities, I had seen how integral family physicians were to the health of these communities. Becoming a "full spectrum" family physician was what I would train for in my residency.

Darlene had already finished two baccalaureate degrees (nutrition sciences and education) with honors, as well as her required dietetic internship. She accepted a position as a dietitian at a hospital in Mississauga, Ontario, a city adjacent to Toronto, far from our roots in the Maritimes. She headed west to start her new life while I finished my last year of medical school. In addition to a lot of clinical learning, the last year involves applying for internships and residency programs. Having asked Darlene to marry me, I ranked Ontario programs high. I was accepted by my first choice, the McMaster University department of family medicine in Hamilton, not far down the highway from Mississauga. After graduating medical school in May, just before my twenty-fifth birthday, I said goodbye to Halifax and moved all of my clothes, my TV, and my Peugeot road bike to Ontario in a newly acquired red sports car to join Darlene.

I was the first of my friends to get married. In celebration with them, I had an over-the-top stag party, arranged by some of my good friends. It started where my romance with Darlene had started—the newspaper storage box, which we saluted with a shot of whiskey. It ended with me being dropped on my parent's front porch in a full body cast. My mother was not impressed. The wedding was on a Saturday afternoon in September, 1991. I remember it all so well: Darlene looking so beautiful in her wedding gown; taking pictures at the Public Gardens in the late afternoon; the reception at the Sheraton ballroom overlooking the harbor; our first dance, to "(Everything I Do) I Do It for You," by Bryan Adams; and, finally, the bridal suite. I was floating in a sea of love all day but I was still able to notice a spark between my best man, Craig, and Darlene's maid of honor, Carol, that would lead us back to the altar eleven months later with our roles reversed.

We rented a townhouse, Darlene's ideal starter home, beside a mall. It was in Burlington, twenty minutes away from my work and around forty from hers—compromises are rarely equal. Being a resident is a grueling job and I frequently worked long hours, with a lot of overnight shifts in the hospital. It was a lonely at times for Darlene, who spent a lot of nights and weekends by herself. When my schedule allowed, we exercised together after work at the local YMCA, a habit that would endure between us.

I was fortunate in my family practice residency. I had a wonderful mentor in Dr. Kenneth Ross Parker, who reinforced the art (as opposed to the science) of medicine. He taught the importance of making patients feel heard and of being accountable to them. He was just what I needed at that stage of my learning. Residency provided me with the skills to help my patients with their problems, whether in the settings of hospital wards, emergency rooms, home visits or the office. I learned to have a "caring ear." In second year, I became one of the chief residents for our unit. I tailored my experiences to help me in community practice, especially in obstetrics, palliative care, and dermatology.

One lasting memory from my residency. An IUD (birth control device) I had inserted in a young mother fell out after two weeks, and we had to meet again for reinsertion. I did this promptly and did not test for pregnancy prior to the procedure. After I had graduated, I got a call from my preceptor telling me that the patient had become pregnant while the IUD was out. Once reinserted, the IUD had gradually enmeshed itself in the growing fetus and by twenty weeks' gestation the pregnancy had to be terminated. She was a lovely young woman and I was devastated to have been the cause of her misfortune. Dr. Parker's advice was to visit her and tell her how sorry I was for what had transpired. I knew that was what I wanted to do and so I met with her and took full responsibility for my mistake, apologized, and told her how horrible I felt. She told me how much the ordeal had affected her. I think it helped her to have her say about the trauma I had unintentionally caused. It certainly humbled me. The actions of physicians can affect lives in dramatic and indelible ways. It is an enormous responsibility and none of us is infallible.

After my residency, I set up a family practice in Georgetown, an hour northwest of downtown Toronto. It was everything we were looking for in a place to live and exactly the type of community hospital I wanted for work: one where family physicians were vital to the function of the hospital and valued by the townspeople. We moved with our two cats into a rental unit while we waited for our house to be built. My first week in the office I saw around ten patients and on Friday evening while walking in the local mall I saw five of them again. You have to love a small town.

My office practice picked up quickly. I stayed open one evening a week for the benefit of my patients, and took regular shifts at the hospital emergency department, not because I loved emergency work but to expand my skill set. I joined the on-call group for the hospital where I would assist after hours for surgeries or when things got busy in the emergency room. There was no pay for being on call. It was expected that you would do it for the community.

I started obstetrics right away and after performing three deliveries under the supervision of our one and only obstetrician, Dr. Valerie Kumar, I started delivering my own patients' babies. Feeling that it was important for a new mother to have a familiar face nearby for such an important life event, I was essentially always on call for my obstetrical patients. Over the years, I was able to attend approximately ninety percent of their births. I also cared for my own hospitalized patients and took over the care of others admitted without a physician. My days and nights were full.

My first major test came in my first October when a three-year-old boy came in by ambulance after being run over on a nearby farm. I was the "lucky" emergency physician. My team quickly put its Advanced Trauma Life Support skills into action and stabilized the boy with bilateral chest tubes for pneumothoraxes. We gave him much-needed IV fluids and stabilized numerous fractures. I took the leadership role and our skilled hospital staff saved this boy's life. After he was stabilized, I accompanied him to McMaster University's pediatric trauma unit by helicopter. This success convinced the emergency nurses and my medical colleagues that I could handle myself when the pressure was on, and from that day forward my emergency skills were sought out in times of critical trauma. I had passed my first test.

Between 1994 and 1997, Darlene and I added three beautiful boys to our family. It was not easy, especially during the early years with the usual sleep deprivation that accompanies young children, but the love that we shared grew exponentially with each addition. I would (much later) share with each of our sons his birth story, starting with our first born, Zachary. I told him all the details, from his first ultrasound to his birth to our first impressions of his character. Benjamin was conceived right around Zach's first birthday and was probably our worst sleeper. I was in a daze of sleep deprivation for all of 1996 and 1997, even though it was Darlene who was up with him most of the time. Just fifteen months later, in October 1997, came Nathaniel. His was a difficult pregnancy for Darlene. She had been hospitalized for extreme abdominal pain and went into labor two weeks earlier than expected but both mother and child came through the birth in good health. Each of our sons had his own unique personality. Zach was determined, persistent and athletic. Ben was a strong, quiet and patient presence. Nathaniel was adventurous, free-spirited and had what Zach called the "cute factor".

With three active young boys our lives were at their busiest. They were all active in team sports, and they skied and snowboarded besides. I tried to keep up with them by playing hockey, snowboarding, golfing, and coaching a lot of their organized activities. On reflection, maybe some part of me knew that I was going to have problems in the future and so I was trying to enjoy time with my boys in a "physical" body as much as I could.

Work also consumed a large amount of time. Life as a full-spectrum family physician in a small town, however rewarding, is one of the most difficult specialties. It requires a vast array of skills. On obstetrics, I could be delivering a baby one minute, and the next resuscitating a newborn and putting in an umbilical vein line to supply it with life-sustaining fluids and medications. In the emergency department, I never knew what would come through the door, and for many evenings and weekends I was the only physician in the building and backup was twenty minutes away. On the inpatient ward, I was on call virtually all the time for my patients, which meant two a.m. calls if one's status suddenly changed. I routinely made house calls to people who could not easily make it to my office. I gave my palliative patients and their families all my contact numbers so they could always reach me.

Given all my duties and responsibilities, and the professional skills required for the range of work I performed, I took great offense when people referred to a family physician as "just a GP." I took a lead role in hospital administration as president of the medical staff and in later years as site Chief of Family Medicine and eventually site Chief of Staff. I was a representative to the GP and Family Practice section of the Ontario Medical Association. My medical practice became a community practice resident teaching site for the University of Toronto. In our community, I was a coach, a Kinsman, and a chalice bearer at St. George's Church. We also had a wide circle of friends that grew as we met new people through the boys' lives.

Eventually, when Nathaniel was two and a half years old, Darlene made the difficult decision to step away from her hospital position. She felt she was not doing either role well with her divided attention.

Fortunately, Darlene never regretted this decision. Selfishly, it helped with my erratic work schedule as dropping off and picking the boys up from the babysitter on the days Darlene worked was no longer a stress. My family always received a large component of my free time but there were periods when my work-life balance was out of whack. Darlene and I were able to talk about these issues before things reached a crisis and I would adjust my schedule. The boys always felt that I was an involved father and Darlene has always felt I was a loving and attentive husband. As the boys got older, Darlene and I started running and going to the gym together again.

I took a moment, on my fortieth birthday, to reflect upon my life. It had involved years of hard work, but with that came great rewards. I had a life partner who made me the best version of myself. We were more in love with each passing year. I had three healthy sons, each developing into his own unique self. I had great relationships with my friends. I was physically fit and healthy. I had a profession that made me feel that I was helping others and that brought me a great sense of self-worth. I was not just content with my life: I loved it, and I was grateful for my good fortune. And then came ALS.

CHAPTER THREE

Living While Dying

WHILE THERE WAS NO way to stop or impede the havoc that ALS would wreak on my body, I did have a window of time before the disease did its worst. Some people have bucket lists or other means of deciding their priorities. I was simply determined to make the most of my available time by cramming in as many moments, meals, trips, and experiences with my young family as I could before I lost the ability to enjoy them.

When I was diagnosed, no one would have been able to tell that I had ALS, and this would be the case for the next year. I chose to let people know of my condition early because I wanted friends, colleagues, and patients to understand why I was gradually reducing my workload and spending more time with my family. I continued exercising at the gym, not to make improvements but to keep the remaining muscle strength that I had for as long as I could. During every workout, I meticulously kept track of my abilities, noting every sign of decline.

I continued my medical practice. Medicine, for me, was always in the "now," and listening to others and helping them with their problems helped me forget about my illness. However, I did slow my activities somewhat over the first year, retiring from my emergency

work—no more scheduled late nights, less body stress. And after ful-
filling promises made to my expectant mothers, I ended obstetrics.
I was losing the finger dexterity required to hand-tie sutures. These
were slight limitations. To people who did not know I had ALS,
I still appeared to be a healthy person.

The psychological toll of giving up my duties was nevertheless
immense; each capitulation to the disease brought feelings of defeat.
My work losses were compounded with the knowledge that ALS had
ended Darlene's entrepreneurial activities. Darlene and our sister-in-
law had started an exciting business of designing and marketing a
line of deluxe baby bags around two years before ALS entered our
lives. Because of my disease, she ended this endeavor and made family her priority. We had our share of tearful moments, and my mind
was sometimes fiercely divided on the question of what was best for
me and my family but for the most part, I was just happy to be alive.

Eighteen months into the illness, in the spring of 2009, I no
longer had the finger dexterity to use scissors with one hand when
assisting in surgery. I suffered some major falls, including one in
which I tripped on a threshold that was an inch above grade and
broke my jaw. This was horrendous for my boys and Darlene to witness, their father and husband bleeding, shaking on the floor, unable
to get up. Fortunately, our friends, the Parkhills, came to our aid and
got me up so that Darlene could take me to the hospital. They also
calmed the boys. This could not have come at a worse time for me
as I was just about to start "voice banking" (a method of recording
that enables your voice to be used in your digital communication
device when you are no longer able to vocalize). Now my normal
voice was lost, as my ability to articulate deteriorated first due to my
fractured jaw and then due to ALS weakening the muscles necessary to enunciate and vocalize. The walker soon followed as I now
feared falling more than I cared about the appearance of using a
walker.

Life was changing quickly, and I had not even reached my forty-third birthday. In the twilight of my career, I was given numerous awards to recognize my contributions. Each award was appreciated but I felt that the honors were premature. The stench of disease accompanied them and, with this, a feeling of unworthiness. I remember being informed, in early May of 2009, that I was going to receive a regional family physician award for the province. I was still able to walk at this time and, half-jokingly, I asked the person who informed me of this award if the stage would be accessible. To my horror, five months later, I received my award totally dependent on a wheelchair. At the end of my second year with ALS, I had to officially retire from clinical practice and end my life's calling. My brain was full of knowledge but my arms no longer had the strength to lift a stethoscope to a patient's chest. I could no longer enunciate clearly and had started using an augmentative speech device because I hated slurring my words and felt that people were judging my intelligence by my inarticulateness. In two years, an active healthy man had been reduced to a severely disabled man.

I remember the last time I cradled a newborn baby, and my last week in the hospital, strolling through the medical unit with a walker to keep my balance—recognizing the irony that my life expectancy was now shorter than that of most of the patients in my charge. On my last day of clinical work, Darlene met me at my office, she walked beside me as I drove my power wheelchair home. The accelerated pace of this disease had caught us unprepared and we had not yet purchased an accessible van for my wheelchair. Two wonderful friends drove close to us during this walk. They recognized that this was the beginning of a "new normal" for us and wanted us to know that they would be there for us when needed. The sky was a brilliant blue at the start of the journey but after five minutes the sky darkened, and we were caught in a thunderstorm. It was hard not to read it as an omen.

With the love and patience of my wife, I continued as the associate chief of staff at my local hospital and helped in the planning of the new emergency department. In the fall of 2011, I officially retired from this hospital leadership position because I felt that to be an effective leader, I had to be a practicing physician. I did not want to go out like a desperate man, clinging to something I had been in the past. I exited when I was still well-regarded and competent. A kind colleague wanted to throw me a retirement party but I immediately shut this down. I did not feel like celebrating a retirement at the age of forty-five when I should yet have been working and contributing. I was more inclined to mourn than to celebrate.

* * *

Throughout this period, our family life looked much as it always had, although our vacation plans were accelerated. I knew travel and many other aspects of life that I enjoyed would be increasingly difficult and, eventually, impossible as the disease progressed. We had some great trips in those years, traveling as a family to the Bahamas and enjoying all the facilities of Atlantis, touring Nashville with Ben's hockey team, with a side trip to Memphis to see Graceland and Beale Street. We went to the Caribbean with our good friends Craig and Carol and their boys. During this cruise, Darlene and I renewed our wedding vows. She was even more beautiful than she had been sixteen years earlier. I had a "stag" party with my boys and Craig and his sons at the ship's arcade, different from my last stag party but probably more meaningful. A still bigger adventure saw our family on a Mediterranean cruise with Craig's family, during which Carol organized a private tour of the attractions of Rome. Even a Protestant like me could be amazed at the aura of the Vatican.

On this trip, I used a scooter and learned that the world is not friendly to the physically disabled. It may look from the outside as though things are accessible but after my son was almost crushed by fast-closing subway doors as I entered a crowded train in Barcelona, and after I almost got dumped into the Grand Canal in Venice while getting onto a water-bus, I found that a lot of accessibility measures are charades. If I am truthful, I was also embarrassed and angry about having to rely on a scooter to get around Europe. You would not know it by looking at me now but I have always been a little vain. How I present to others matters to me. ALS is not kind to a person's appearance. I once resented this. It took time to accept that I no longer have much of an appearance to be vain about.

With other friends, we visited New York City at Christmastime and saw the holiday splendors of that city. Later we explored Washington, DC, toured the White House, and got lost in the many Smithsonian museums along the Mall. We saw Spain and Morocco, shopping in the Algiers market where we negotiated for a handmade rug, stopping by the Casbah, and going to the coast where we rode camels. I relished every meal, knowing that before long I would be fed through a tube.

We also had the opportunity to spend time with my own extended family. My parents gave my brothers and me a gift of travel money so that we could make a trip with them to Florida. We took a picture of all of us in front of my parents' rented villa. This would be the last photo of all of my siblings and their spouses and children. With my brothers' families, we visited Disney World. I have a vivid memory of being on the Dumbo ride with fireworks exploding in the background, a surprisingly magical experience. Darlene and I also made it to Halifax to celebrate my father's accomplishments as an engineer at a gala in his honor. I stayed for an extra week and walked for the last time through the city, through my old neighborhood, through the university where I had given tours twenty years before, knowing that it would be my last unaided walk along familiar paths. At the end of the week, I showed some of my friends from Ontario the pleasures of a Halifax pub crawl.

There were other trips: to Vancouver, and then Whistler to visit my brother Brent and his family; to reunions in Mont-Tremblant and Boston with my friends from school days; to Prince Edward Island with still more friends and family; to Toronto for a weekend with my medical friends, followed by another reunion with them in Montreal. We continued to go for a four-day vacation every August to Tippecanoe Lake in Indiana, where our friends have a cottage. With four families visiting this cottage every year for ten years, we saw all of our children grow and become young adults. The kids were exposed to tube rides, water-skiing, wakeboarding, wave runners, and "extreme" croquet. The pontoon-boat rides around the lake are etched in my memory.

To some extent, these excursions and reunions were made possible by my disease. Illness brings a sense of urgency to relationships and makes you want to celebrate them. I am grateful to the friends and family who accompanied us on all our adventures. They helped Darlene, the boys, and me cope with my physical losses by treating us as we wanted to be treated—as a family still living graceful and energetic lives. I realized that being a friend is about appreciating every large or small sacrifice someone makes to enhance the richness of your life; I learned to be a better friend through those shared adventures.

I enjoyed our experiences but my knowledge of what the disease had in store for me somewhat lessened my ability to be fully joyful and, as the disease progressed, my disabilities prohibited me from fully engaging in activities. I was not able to join my boys on the Whistler ski hill. I sat outside the ruins of Pompeii while the rest of my family toured this once great city. Often my inability to participate also meant Darlene's exclusion from activities. By the time we went back to the Caribbean in 2010, our final cruise, I was in my wheelchair and our new realities broke wide open. We were frustrated with how airport security treated the disabled, and the non-accessibility of the cruise line. We were stuck in an accessible bus for an hour before the boat left the dock. Both my chair and my communications device broke down in passage. Fortunately, we were traveling with three other families who did not hesitate to take our boys with them on excursions when I was prevented from participating. Each time the boys departed without us, they would make sure we were okay with them going. The reality and sadness of the situation was palpable to everyone no matter how often Darlene and I told them we were perfectly okay with it. We were faced, cruelly and unavoidably, with how different we were from everyone else on the ship because of my disabilities. As difficult as these moments were, I was further distressed by the knowledge that I would never be able to repeat them.

* * *

Although we packed the years between 2009 and 2014 with all we could manage and held on to as much normality as we could, remaining (for the most part) positive and hopeful, to shelter the boys from my illness, we all had to adapt to living with disability. I was slowly becoming inanimate. From losing finger strength and dexterity, making buttons and zippers difficult to manipulate, to losing complete control of my hands, my arms, and my legs, to losing my abilities to speak, to sing, to chew and to swallow, I became physically dependent on others. Toward the end of that time, I needed someone to wipe my bottom and scratch any itch. Darlene had to pivot-transfer me into bed in the evening and out again in the morning. I was able to be pivot-transferred because I still had residual strength in my legs and Darlene, although just five foot two, is remarkably strong. As my legs weakened, she took more of my weight. Her back paid the price so we began to ask one of the boys, who were becoming strong young men, to help when possible.

There were new vulnerabilities to contend with. I had two separate episodes of severe choking on food, during which Zach on the first episode and Craig on the second had to wrap their arms around me and pull upward from behind to clear my upper airway. The risk of blocking my airway increased with my inability to synchronize the muscles involved with swallowing, so I altered the texture of my diet. At the same time, I could not lift my hands to feed myself so I had to be spoon-fed. My food was mashed together and mixed with gravy. The energy required to eat was taxing me and I started to lose weight as my oral intake could no longer keep up with my energy needs.

There were episodes when vomit refluxed onto my vocal cords causing my trachea to go into spasm and necessitating Darlene to suction my airway for hours to prevent aspiration. The pressure on Darlene to keep me alive in these moments was tremendous. The episodes were exhausting for both of us. Constipation was another frequent problem. I was reluctant to use too much laxative for fear of accidents and as a result I could be on the toilet for hours waiting to pass large, hard claylike stools.

Three years after my diagnosis, I decided to have my first life-prolonging intervention, a tube in my abdomen that provided an entry directly to my stomach to provide nourishment. I reflected that seventy years ago Lou Gehrig did not have this workaround procedure. It would not be correct to call it a treatment. I was amazed that medical science has made such incredible progress on practically every disease confronting humans yet no progress in the treatment of ALS and many other neurodegenerative diseases since Gehrig's time. My last meal was around a year later, a Dairy Queen banana split that I shared with Darlene.

I could still breathe on my own although at night I used a BiPap machine, a type of ventilator that pushes air through a mask into your airways, opening your lungs, making it easier to breathe. I drooled all the time and after exhausting medication remedies I tried radiation therapy and Botox injections on my salivary glands in an attempt to slow them down. The traveling back and forth to receive these treatments—full-day excursions—was exhausting for Darlene. Fortunately, our friends helped with driving on a few of these trips. None of the therapies had a great effect on my drooling and I continue to drool excessively.

Our house had to be changed to make it accessible. With the financial help of my parents, an elevator was installed. Fortunately, it became operational the day that I could no longer climb the stairs to our bedroom. The elevator allowed us the luxury of not making our living room into a bedroom and having the whole house appear as a hospital ward. Darlene and I also converted a bathroom to make it accessible and put a large ramp into our family room so that I could enter and exit the house through the garage. All these changes, although costly, reinforced the idea that we would coexist with ALS in as normal an environment as possible, that we were in it for the long run and, most important, that the boys would not have to be removed from their neighborhood and their treasured friends.

Darlene was becoming my full-time caregiver. She took care of all my feeding and suction requirements, turning me at night in bed, toileting, and showering, all while still caring for the boys, on minimal sleep. I was waking up frequently, which added to her sleep deprivation. Seeing this play out was hard on us both. The boys stepped up whenever asked and through their teenage years never caused us major problems. When their mom had to run errands, I was always amazed at their ability to care for me. They were given more chores than their friends and rarely complained because they wanted to help their mother as much as they could.

My only means of communication was by now with my eyes, picking out letters and words on a screen mounted eighteen inches in front of my face. My eyes were my independence, their muscles the only ones I could voluntarily control. With my eyes and the wonder of technology, I could speak, write, learn, teach, and explore the world via the Internet.

The technology is great until it shuts down inexplicably, as all computers do from time to time. Sometimes there is an easy fix, requiring only that someone notice the computer is not working and then turn it off and back on, or call for support (usually a two-hour experience). Far too often, it needs to be serviced externally, taking three to five days during which I am unable to work or express myself. These episodes are infuriating and exhausting for us. I am even more helpless than usual and Darlene has to be hypervigilant because I am unable to express my needs. The fragile peace we have made with ALS is shattered and a foul atmosphere descends upon our home. My technology and access to the Internet are vital to life within the horrendous physical restrictions of ALS. Without them, I would have passed on three years into the disease. I am reminded every time the computer shuts down what life is like for ALS sufferers unable to afford the technology (some health plans do not cover these devices, even in Canada).

This was my status until August 2014 when I suddenly had to be admitted to the hospital.

CHAPTER FOUR

When You Stop Breathing

THE TROUBLE STARTED WITH a rash on my lower back, a low fever, and a feeding-tube blockage. I also noticed that I was unusually short of breath after my son Zach had lifted me from bed to wheelchair. The rash and the fever were still there the next day and I was off to the emergency room. With Darlene and Zach by my side, I was told that they had found changes in my blood work that meant I would have to be admitted. In the early evening, Nathaniel and his girlfriend Erica visited and Ben had the misfortune of visiting a little later, during which I had a bowel movement while I was in my chair. Ben and Darlene cleaned me up and got me ready for bed. That evening I e-mailed Darlene my preferred funeral arrangements. I had an intuition that something was about to happen to me.

I slept reasonably well that night. I had a private nurse so Darlene was also able to get some rest, worry-free. The next morning, Darlene came to the hospital to prepare for a normal day. As she was transferring me to the commode chair I felt my tongue roll back and block my airway. I did not have the strength to breathe. Darlene knew something was wrong and quickly put me back to bed and called for help.

I knew I could not breathe but I was conscious and my mind could follow what was going on around me. I heard Darlene say, "I am not ready to lose him." The blood beating in my eardrums was extremely loud. I remember thinking, *Well, this sucks.* I do not remember being sad. I was angry that I was going to die over something as prosaic as being moved to the commode. I did not see my life pass before my eyes but I did see the profile of a young boy, not recognizable as myself or one of my sons. My mind gave him the name Josh. Upon that last visualization, my mind went black.

Darlene had seen my family physician and good friend Dr. Wei Chu at the nurses' station when coming to my room. She ran out and called for him and while he was assessing my condition, Darlene suggested they put me on the BiPap while waiting for the crash cart. I think this saved my life because I was regaining consciousness slowly and I remember thinking, *Don't take me off this, it's working.* They did take me off it and again everything went black until I awoke an hour later in the intensive care unit with a breathing tube down my throat. Unbeknownst to me, when I was unconscious Wei persistently "bagged" me, squeezing air into my lungs for forty-five minutes. It was because of his skill that I did not suffer any damage from inadequate oxygenation during this incident.

I knew, on waking, that I had endured a near-death experience. Oddly, it did not meet my expectations. Why had I not been granted the spiritual experience of a bright light to guide me, as have many others in similar circumstances? Why had I not felt myself hovering above my body? I had seen that silhouette of a boy but I could not explain to myself why everything afterward went black. I had felt sad, alone, and afraid, and an eternity passed before I opened my eyes again. I was so disappointed by that blackness that my belief in a spiritual life after death was almost extinguished. Maybe when we die we just die, I thought, and nothing exists after physical life.

Although the decision to be intubated for support of my breathing was somewhat forced upon me by my sudden respiratory arrest, I had long been prepared for the inevitability. Knowing I would eventually lose my ability to breathe, I had decided after much internal debate to keep living regardless. In the spring of 2009, Darlene and I saw a respirologist to discuss my future needs. He thought we would be foolish to consider prolonging a life with ALS and went on to detail what that would entail. As we continued to see him throughout the worsening of the illness and he saw that we were coping reasonably well within the confines of a severely restricted disease, he seemed to relent in his objections, or at least to become convinced that I was not going to change my mind. He arranged for us to see an otolaryngologist, or head and neck specialist, in the spring of 2014.

At that appointment, we discussed a tracheotomy, a procedure which meant I would cede control of my lungs to an external ventilator attached through a tube in my neck. The physician wanted to know if we understood what we were getting ourselves into with so invasive a measure. By that stage, however, I had lost virtually all of my muscle control and I felt that my disability could not get much worse. A tracheotomy would even have some beneficial side effects: I would not have to constantly protect my airway from accidental swallowing of saliva into my trachea. When that happened, as it regularly did, Darlene had to deep-suction my airway on and off for an hour, physically exhausting for me and mentally exhausting for her as my life hung in the balance during these episodes. The tracheotomy could mean a better quality of life for both of us.

Another reason I felt a permanent airway would help was that I was increasingly unproductive as breathing became more difficult. I had been writing a lot prior to 2014 but my energy had since waned.

My resting heart rate was consistently in the low 110s (normally a resting heart rate would be between 60 and 80), as if I had just run five kilometers when all I was doing was sitting in my wheelchair, breathing. There were also increasing episodes when I was not tolerating my feed well, I would become extremely hot and my heart rate would jump into the 120s. My body could not digest food and breathe at the same time without my heart working harder.

What's more, I was tired of the BiPap. I had used it every night for four years. I recalled putting patients with severe congestive heart failure on BiPap when I worked in emergency. I had always apologized to them because while it is considered a non-invasive measure it was akin to torture in my eyes. The high pressures and the need for a fit around the nose and mouth without air leaks mean it is very uncomfortable. For me, it caused skin ulcers on the bridge of my nose, a very dry mouth, and a claustrophobic feeling. I needed it because it was prolonging my life but it was less than ideal. In my opinion, any ALS patient wanting to live with the disease as comfortably as possible requires a tracheostomy (the name for the opening created by a tracheotomy, through which the ventilator is inserted) when things deteriorate to the point of needing full-time BiPap support.

I have been on the ventilator ever since my respiratory arrest and I now have much better control of my airway. I also have a clear and direct route through my tracheostomy to suction my trachea and prevent the occurrence of pneumonia from my oral secretions. Tracheostomies and ventilators are hardly cures for ALS but they do provide a dramatic example of how technology can prolong a life. That said, they should only be considered after a quality-of-life review with the patient and his or her family and primary caregivers. A decision to live with a respirator is a decision to accept artificial life support over the long term, and it may not be for everyone. My decision did not come easily.

I went back and forth on the advisability of the procedure, worrying about the effect it would have on my family. It was a difficult decision and there were moments when I wished that I would die before having to make choices about my continued existence. I was concerned primarily for Darlene. I felt that the longer I lived, the harder it would be for her to find a future partner with whom she could live in a world without ALS. Choosing to live with a ventilator would have less of a negative impact on my boys, who were increasingly independent. I knew that my choosing to live would not greatly decrease the quality of their lives because they only occasionally had to help with my care needs; Darlene performed most of my care and was the person most limited by my disease. Concern for her was my largest position against living.

In the other column were a number of considerations, starting with the simple fact that my stubborn body and mind refused to quit. I knew there would come a time when they would just give up, and I believed that time was near, but it had not yet arrived. I was relatively young for someone with ALS. I was not suffering, I had no physical pain, and I was free of the mental disease that people often associate with my level of disability. I had already adapted to my change in physical abilities by using new technologies that improved the quality and quantity of my life. I had learned to accept help for all my daily activities, and I was reconciled to living out the rest of my life dependent on others for everything except the environment that I could control with my eyes and my screen. Some of the "dying with dignity" advocates think that a person could never live with dignity if he or she needs to rely on others to perform all their care needs. I have learned that I can maintain my dignity by caring for people in other ways. Through being kind, appreciative, attentive, and supportive, I have found great self-worth.

Fortunately, I knew that my living would not cause excessive financial hardship to my family, as is often the case with ALS. It is an incredibly expensive illness. Forty percent of people who are diagnosed with ALS live in poverty. We have paid close to $250,000 in ALS-related bills to cover home modifications; accessible vans, wheelchairs, and scooters; communications devices; and miscellaneous health care costs not covered by insurance. All this while living in a country with a public health system, supplemented by my private health insurance and disability insurance coverage. Yet until I reach sixty-five, I am able to support my family comfortably and save money for retirement through a well-designed disability-insurance plan that brings in close to what I was making as a family physician. I have health insurance that pays for my medication and for my nursing services above my provincial home care support services. Finally, when I do pass away, we will have a paid-off home, retirement savings, and life insurance that will provide the stability my wife and sons will need. Having this in place alleviated my fear of living by artificial means and becoming a financial burden on my family.

There was also the fact that I *wanted* to live. I am not going to preach that attitude can help all diseases and delay the inevitable but I have witnessed firsthand when giving palliative care that some people can will themselves to one more birthday or holiday while others can push themselves to a speedy death. Most importantly, attitude does affect the quality of your remaining life and that of your family.

Finally, and most important to me, was my family. What really kept me here, and still does, is the feeling that I am loved by Darlene and my boys. Without them in my life, there would be no reason to fight on. I enjoy watching the boys grow and I want to be around for their futures. My guilt about impinging on Darlene's future happiness has been assuaged as time has passed through the help of external care providers. She is not always required to put her life on hold to care for my endless needs. She can concentrate on her own care at least for a few hours and I feel like much less of a burden on her. I have also developed a trust in the divinity of the universe that tells me I will physically die when my life's purposes have been fulfilled.

All those realities fed into my decision to keep living with ALS—to adapt to the disease rather than wait to die. I would accept my limitations, rely upon assistive treatments and devices to improve my circumstances, and, aided by the good graces of my family and caregivers, make the best of things. Others with the same disease but different circumstances have and will continue to choose other ways that they think are best for them or their family. Having sat on both sides of the desk, I understand and support their personal decisions.

CHAPTER FIVE

A Day in the Life

BEFORE ALS, I WAS A sound sleeper. Not anymore. With my body getting tired of its position, I wake at two forty-five a.m. I have a nurse watching me as I sleep and have my head positioned so that she can see my eyes open. Being unable to utter a sound, this is the only signal I can give that my body needs a position change. Because I still have my sense of touch, I am vulnerable to the usual discomforts of remaining too long in one recumbent position. I turn my head an inch to the right and the nurse knows that this subtle movement means I want to be turned on my right side. Pillows are rearranged so that can be done. A long pillow is placed along my back and buttocks. This props me on my side. Another pillow is placed between my lower legs and feet with my knees bent at around thirty degrees. The last pillow is placed in front of me and my arm is placed on it with a slight bend at my elbow.

I keep my eyes closed throughout this procedure because if I open them, I get overstimulated and have problems falling back to sleep. When the nurse asks, "Is your head okay?" I raise my eyebrows to reply yes. The question is then repeated for each body part—arms, buttocks, legs—and my response is given with an eyebrow raise or the absence of an eyebrow raise, signaling a reposition is necessary.

You might think I am being obsessive about my position but even in my drugged state, my position dictates whether I will sleep for another two hours or will have to repeat all this in less than an hour.

At four thirty, I am awake again. In this position, my head is turned away from the nurse. Fortunately, I am still able to straighten my legs thanks to a residual twenty percent of my original muscle mass in my thighs and buttocks. This is my second signal to my nurse that I need to turn. I am placed back in my original position, flat on my back, and my pillows are repositioned so that my feet and arms are supported. This time when my head is moved, the rumble of misdirected saliva can be heard in my tracheostomy tube. I cough and hypersalivate, and the nurse quickly redirects her attention to clearing my obstructed airway. The loud suction machine is turned on and my airway and mouth are vacuumed out. During the tracheostomy suctioning, the tube is opened and the alarm on my ventilator chimes in protest. If I am lucky, my teeth do not bite down on my tongue during my frequent suction-induced coughing fits.

The arousal from the suctioning means that the turns and my sleep will shorten to segments of an hour or ninety minutes. During these segments, I dream. My most frequent recurrent dream takes me back to when I am not quite yet a physician. In my dream, I have some health problem in residency that keeps me from finishing my program. This dream restates to me the reality of my life. I am not quite a physician anymore.

I am usually fully awake by seven thirty. By this time my night nurse has left, and Darlene is in the room watching for me to stir. When I wake, my head is usually turned away from Darlene and my legs are fully straightened. I have no way to allow Darlene to know that I am awake except for a subtle head turn that she can notice only if she happens to be looking at me directly. This is the time I hate because I feel the full force of gravity pinning me to the mattress. Thankfully, Darlene is quick in coming to my rescue. She removes

the pillows, repositions me, and gets the urinal so I can relieve my
full bladder. Once this is done, I can relax and think about the day
before me. Darlene opens the blinds of my large window and I feel
the heaviness of Lily, our cockapoo, on my legs. Lily was a puppy
when I first had to use a wheelchair. She has brought so much joy
into our lives through the turmoil of ALS. We both like to look out
at the hummingbirds, chickadees, and squirrels that frequent the
bird feeders Ben has put outside my window. Occasionally, we will
see a messenger in the form of a cardinal, blue jay, or oriole. When
I see them, my spirit is lifted.

My support workers start at either eight or nine every morning.
On the days when they come later, Darlene will pull my slider sheet
so that she has room to crawl into bed beside me. She will turn my
head so that we are looking at each other. As with most turns of my
head, I will require suction of my tracheostomy and my mouth.
When Darlene does join me in bed and wraps her body around
mine it is invariably the best part of the morning. We do a guided
meditation together to start our day in a peaceful state.

The active part of my day starts as my support worker greets me,
"Good morning, Jeff!" I respond with a blink of my eyes and what I
imagine is a smile but is probably a grimace. Pulling down my warm
blanket, she exposes my upper abdomen where my gastronomy tube
sticks out like a valve on an air mattress. She connects a tube to the
valve and boluses my crushed morning medications and my morning feed into my stomach with six, 60 ml syringes. This takes around
five minutes to complete. I was a quick eater before ALS but this is
fast even for me.

When my feed is resting comfortably in my stomach, my exercising begins. Starting with my legs, then my arms and hands,
every major joint is moved. I credit this workout for preventing my
extremities from having the same sort of contractures that contorted
Stephen Hawking's body, and for sparing me the pain that can come

with ALS. With my workout complete, Darlene will join the support worker to help me dress and transfer me to my wheelchair. If I have had gas, I will have fouled the gym shorts in which I sleep. Darlene cleans this up and helps pull up my pants. I go commando now. I've opted out of underwear because one less layer of clothing makes it easier for my support workers and Darlene to help me pee. This has reduced wetness in my genital area dramatically. After my pants are on, I am transferred from my bed to my wheelchair. I wear regular, nonmodified clothing and am most comfortable in jeans. I do the transfer with a ceiling lift and sling. Unfortunately movement exacerbates the blockage of my tracheostomy so these activities are frequently interrupted by suction.

You might be wondering when I shower and go to the bathroom. Two days a week, I forgo my exercises and am "primed" for toileting and the shower. It is quite an adventure. Two days before, I start a regimen of laxatives so that I am ready for optimal evacuation. On the appropriate day, I am transferred onto my tilt commode. I am given a suppository and then I feed while over the toilet. My feed with some green tea helps to stimulate the gastrocolic reflex and helps me have a bowel movement. Usually I do my business within thirty minutes, get cleaned up, and am rolled into the shower. For the sake of modesty, I have a facecloth covering my pubic area. I love hot showers and the sensation of the water hitting my skin. For my first nine years of having ALS, Darlene would do my toileting and shower. For the last three years, she has been able to give these chores to my support workers, which is a relief for her.

In my power wheelchair, I am ready to finish my dressing (back to a non-shower day). As if I were a puppet, my left arm is raised and released from my nightshirt. My right arm does the same and my puppet masters are now able to remove the whole shirt. This show is continued for my deodorant, a new T-shirt, and a sweater. Next is the adjustment of my position in my chair. Positioning is the most important thing in my day. If I am able to maintain a good posture in my chair, I can have a productive day and use my computer with ease. If I do not have the position correct, my day is relegated to passive activities. Fortunately, this is a rare event.

I have my teeth brushed, my face shaved and washed, and now, two hours after this process with my support worker has begun, I am ready to spend the next eleven or twelve hours upright in my chair in our living room. And I can now talk again.

My ventilation machine is small enough to fit onto the back of my wheelchair, enabling me to move from room to room. The screen in front of my face is a Microsoft Surface tablet. Attached to the bottom of the tablet is a Tobii miniature eye-tracker. This, with my Tobii software, allows my eye movement to interface with my computer. My eyes are my mouse. By staring at a letter for a half-second, my "dwell" setting will automatically "enter" the letter, the word-predicted "word" or anything else that my eyes target. This is why positioning in my chair is so important. If I am seated in my chair a centimeter too far to one side or the other, I cannot be as precise with the eye-tracker. Getting a tracheostomy suction or even yawning can also knock me out of position. Fortunately, we are masters at getting my positioning right and I can usually make the most of my technology. It's not easy but with ten thousand hours of practice under my belt, I am now an eye-tracking expert, able to type fifteen words a minute. I like to think this is my superpower. I can do all of what most people can do with a computer. I can communicate, control my environment, including my television and music systems, and independently choose what I want from the digital world, shopping or making calls with my home assistant devices. I know that without these technologies, had I simply been "locked in" to my paralyzed body, I would not have chosen to live. The development of the Internet has made a huge difference in the quality of life of severely disabled patients.

My days vary from this time on, depending upon the time of year and the projects in which I am involved. Also, while most days I require tracheostomy suction ten to fifteen times, other days it can be incessant, reaching twenty to thirty times during the twelve hours I am in my chair (the amount of suctioning required is highly variable for each person with ALS). Tracheostomy suction may sound terrible and my grimace and cough may make it appear as though I am being tortured but it does not cause me any pain. The cough that it induces, which helps bring up the phlegm obstructing my tube, makes my muscles go into an involuntary extension spasm. If you have witnessed a seizure, my body goes into a similar state. I used to slide in my wheelchair a lot with this. Now, whenever I get tracheostomy suction I have my feet strapped to my footrests and this keeps me in position.

I have a constant companion with me during the days and evenings. For the first nine years of my illness, Darlene or one of my sons did ninety percent of this work. Since Darlene has accepted more help, she spends half of her time with me and is able to devote more time to self-care during the rest of the day.

I like to be productive in my chair. Like everyone else, I start the day by looking at my e-mails. I decide what needs a quick answer and what needs a more thoughtful reply. After that first glance at the inbox, I put on some music. My house is wired for sound. Through the use of my Bose sound system and my streaming service, I am able to impose my eclectic musical taste on everyone on the premises. You can find me listening to Lou Reed, the Beatles, Stan Rogers, Ed Sheeran, Pink Floyd, the Eagles, or Frank Sinatra at any given moment. When I'm feeling reflective, John Denver, Rush, and Simon and Garfunkel help me through the day. Music is like a time machine for me, taking me out of my current body back to a time when I had a working body.

I always have some kind of project on the go. I tend not to waste my day binging on Netflix. I enjoy reading nonfiction, testing my scientific mind to the extreme with the theories of quantum physics (I have not mastered the subject, but then no one has). I also enjoy reading about the past through biographies. I dabble in the stock market, enjoying the highs and berating myself during the lows for not having sold. I think a knowledge of the financial system is important for all of us if only to follow your retirement savings. I have an insatiable appetite for the news, and I am always on the lookout for a variety of opinions on stories that interest me.

During the springtime, I am busy fund-raising for the Walk to End ALS. I take the time to write everyone who has supported me to thank them for their generosity. Given that the illness has a high five-year mortality rate, there are few of us "Champions of ALS" around. I continue to be amazed and humbled by the generous support my community and donors show for the people and their families who have had ALS enter their lives.

In the summer, I get out as much as I can. Because my neck is too weak to hold up my head, I wear a baseball cap out-of-doors with a shoelace connecting the back of the hat to my headrest pole. I am lucky to now live on a riverside property surrounded by nature. I enjoy being totally immersed in it while the weather is mild. The other eight months of the year, I can only watch from afar.

As my Facebook friends can attest, I do not have much of a social media presence. The feed of Facebook leads me down the rabbit hole of personal scarcity: I get down because I do not have the same pictures of great times to share. I still have great times but the pictures of these events remind me of how different our lives are from most. Recently, I have started coaching friends and others with the help of Darlene who has become a certified life coach. This has been especially meaningful to me as I'm now able to more formally engage in helping others. I am moving forward with my primary purpose in life.

The bolus feeds continue throughout the day until I get my daily 1,500 calories of nutrition and plenty of water. The urinal usage continues and, if I'm lucky, I can get through the day without any urine spilled upon me. The evening is a time of connection for Darlene and me, our alone time when we can talk about our day and make sure we are both feeling well. After Darlene gets dinner over with and the other chores done for the night, we unwind with a TV show or movie. We particularly enjoy watching our professional sports teams and sappy romantic dramas. I like to think my taste for sappy romantic dramas is because ALS has made my brain soft but the truth is I have always enjoyed them. I will usually cry for a moment after these shows. Darlene is always there to wipe away my tears. I don't know why they make me cry now when they rarely did before the illness. I can only surmise that the adversities suffered by the characters allow me to mourn my own losses. The shows are probably a good way for me to let go.

At ten each night, Darlene gets busy again and brushes my teeth and combs my hair. The feeling of the comb's teeth on my scalp is wonderful for a man unable to scratch. She prepares my last syringe for the night. It contains enough sleeping medication to knock me out within five minutes of hitting my mattress. The night nurse has arrived. I use my voice-bank files and say in my pre-ALS voice: "I love you, Zach. I love you, Ben. I love you, Nathaniel. I love you, Darlene. Good night. Love you." Darlene turns off my voice and drives me to my bedroom. I hear classical music as my puppet arms are lifted up to get my sweater off. The sling is put around my body and I'm lifted from my wheelchair into my hospital bed. Darlene and the nurse discretely remove my jeans and put on my athletic shorts. "Good night, honey," says Darlene, and gives me a kiss. Tracheostomy suction is the last thing I remember.

CHAPTER SIX

Who Your Friends Are

I N ADDITION TO THE restrictions that a serious disease puts on a couple are the restrictions a couple puts upon itself when faced with severe disability. For instance, Darlene and I decided to opt out of the "real world" as much as possible as my limitations increased. When we did leave our home, Darlene felt like the center of attention, which she detests, and because of the limitations of my communications technology my abilities out-of-doors deteriorated to the point where I felt totally incapable (my communication device doesn't work in the direct sun). These experiences were so discouraging that our outings became less and less frequent and are now limited to trips to the hospital for tracheostomy changes and a limited number of other excursions each year.

That is one way we have limited ourselves somewhat more than the disease has limited us. Darlene and I live in a cocoon built for our own protection. It consists of our house and our yard. Within it, we have the illusion of normality, and who does not want to feel normal? We are also shielded from the fear of missing out. We do not come across the mass of people living the life that twelve years ago we felt we were entitled to as well. Over time, we have been working on our phobias and are adjusting ourselves psychologically to living in a far-from-normal state. We are still most comfortable at home entertaining friends.

A cocoon creates a buffer against the external world but it cannot protect you from everything. It cannot protect you from what goes on in your own head—your personal thoughts and feelings about your circumstances. From the moment of my diagnosis with this illness, life has been tainted with the questions, *Why us?* and *What would our lives be like if we were living without profound loss?* While the questions remain largely unspoken because to utter them too frequently would demean the attempt to live in the present, I cannot help but think of the circumstances of my imprisonment. "I haven't done anything," I plead. "I am innocent." Of course these words, expressed only to myself on the feeling-sorry-for-myself mornings as I lie awake in bed, do no good.

During my first seven years of illness, when Darlene was caring for me around the clock, she had words of her own on those days. "I hate what I have become," she would say. "I feel guilty all of the time." This is the toll ALS puts on a couple. My brain interpreted her feelings as a single message: *The breaks are not long enough and now I feel lost in the forever of our situation.* As she has accepted more help, her feelings of selfhood have improved but her guilt is still present. My happiness is unfairly derived from her happiness. When she is not happy, I feel personally responsible for every tear that falls. When I hear or feel her thinking negative thoughts I wonder if continuing in my limited existence is worth making two lives miserable. My guilt is overwhelming. I am the obstacle to her being physically hugged, kissed, and caressed by a normal husband. She, too, feels guilt—the guilt of the able person in the presence of extreme disability.

Meanwhile, my friends and peers are at the peak of their careers, each one climbing higher on the ladder of success, reaching further in pursuits far beyond my present abilities. You would think I would be jealous of almost all my peers and, indeed, some days this ugly emotion does poke its head up. I can envy people who are unscathed in life and living as I thought I was entitled to live. I do miss the events I see others participating in, such as winter getaways, trips for special anniversaries, and simple activities like running with my wife. Am I jealous of them or merely feeling like I am missing out on a good time? I am not sure. That is one of the ambiguities of my current state.

There are occasionally people who do not seem to be living good lives, as I have tried to live, and I cannot help but think, *Why am I being punished with a debilitating disease and why do they seem to have everything? Why do some seemingly unaccountable people get to live their dreams when my dreams have been derailed, now and forever?* I know that by thinking this way I am slipping into the negative state of judgment, which I now recognize as a great character flaw. Realizing that this is not a good state of mind, I do not linger in it. if I did, I could not survive. Instead I try to give, which provides me with my best sense of self-worth. I guess that is why I miss my original calling so much—my practice was a form of giving and it made me a very happy individual.

Many of my friends and peers have been incredibly supportive and have stayed in my life throughout my illness, and some friendships have strengthened as I have weakened. In other instances, relationships have changed for the worse. Connections that I thought would never be compromised by illness are gone forever. We have had friends, very important people in our lives, who were strong during a point in my illness when I needed them most but who, over time, separated themselves from us. I have always tried to remain as positive as I can among friends, knowing that being moody and sad does not meet the unwritten friendship rules. Nevertheless, some people cannot deal with my new realities, cannot see past my frail physical appearance. Perhaps they have their own insecurities about illness or want to protect themselves from further loss upon my inevitable passing. It has still hurt me. Abandonment at a time of need is something I do not understand, especially when I have seen other relationships flourish under difficult circumstances.

Early in my disease, as its progress was becoming more visible to the outside world, I lost one particularly close support within my family. The disintegration of this relationship hit me and my family hard. After my diagnosis, my extended family celebrated Christmas together for the first time in many years and, as mentioned, we all got together again with my parents in Florida in the winter of 2009. Although I was wrapped in support during this trip, I sensed a change with my older brother. Our relationship became awkward and it has stayed that way.

Friends can leave one's life relatively easily: the only difficulty is a by-chance meeting at the local gathering place, an arena, or a store. When family decide to exit your lives, the leaving is never complete. There will be situations in the future where family members will have to be in the same room with one another and their hurt feelings will only gather strength. When families partially break up, other members of the family take sides and further fracturing occurs.

I believe these matters can be reduced to an equation: family dysfunction is directly proportional to the degree of tragedy that a family experiences. Most families function well when no adversity is faced. The small tensions that exist stay small. When a close tragedy occurs, instead of "rallying around the family" as the feel-good movies show us, the opposite usually occurs. The tensions accumulate and metastasize, as they did in my family despite best efforts from myself. In this instance (there are others to come), I wrote directly to family members, raising my concerns, trying always to address the elephant in the room. Nothing changed. Ultimately, we had to estrange ourselves from this relationship because to continue the charade only made the sting of abandonment more painful for me and my family.

I know we did not always deal with abandonment well. At times, we passed judgment and shame. We cannot always take the high road when faced with sudden and continual change. If I were on the other side of the relationship, I would hope that I would give grace points to those most affected by the circumstances. I like to think that when concerns about a relationship were raised, I would have the compassion to pull the wounded toward me and not push them away. Not everyone thinks this way, however, and now some of our relationships are probably irreparable. Friendships and family relationships require unconditional love to thrive. Loving opens us all to hurt when the loved one leaves, whether the leaving is physical or emotional. Some people seek to protect themselves from this eventual hurt proactively. I suggest that by doing this you are missing out on the gift of life, the acknowledgment of the preciousness of health and love, of how giving to those in need is actually a gift to yourself.

Unfortunately, the simple truth is that with any tragic loss you face, more loss will follow. The best way forward is to accept this as inevitable. "Say goodbye and wish them well", says Rush lyricist Neil Peart. Concentrate on strengthening those relationships that remain. Adaptation is the key to survival.

CHAPTER SEVEN

Missing Movement

YEARS OF LIVING WITH my disease, and years of having been transported from location to location like a rock in a wheelbarrow, have given me time to think about what I miss most from my former life. Perhaps surprisingly it is not the glamorous travel or the complexities of being a hospital chief of staff. It is often the simple pleasures, things that many able people take for granted. I do not like to dwell upon what I miss but I do think that writing about it allows a better understanding of the many facets of this illness. Some of my losses are specific to ALS, but many are relatable to any person or family living with terminal illness.

I miss dreaming of the future. Immediately after diagnosis, I knew that my and Darlene's expected future vision of our lives had evaporated. Our expectations of living the lives that so many take for granted abruptly stopped on that day. I was likely to die at a young age. Darlene would be a widow at a young age. There was no future for us that did not include hardship and incredible adversity. We would not be able to fully enjoy life because my impending disability and death would be conjoined with any future good times. I would not be able to have my own dreams because I had just reached the precipice of my life and I was now on a fast descent. The world is for a person who is able to move. I still have dreams for my future but they are not personal dreams so much as dreams for the well-being and happiness of the people I love.

I miss physical contact, from holding hands to more intimate contact with the one I love. I miss it all. Intimacy expressed between friends and acquaintances could include a handshake, a pat on the back, a hug, or a kiss on the cheek. Now there seems to be an invisible barrier around me that prevents me from receiving these gestures from all but my closest family and friends. Intimacy between a couple includes holding hands, hugs, kisses, and the more intimate touching that other couples take for granted and that Darlene and I no longer experience together. One of the cruel ironies of this disease is that I still have the ability to have erections because the involuntary smooth muscles of the penis are not affected. I also retain a sex drive. With the increasing time in the wheelchair, my sensitivity has been affected to the point that my orgasms are difficult to attain and the pleasure sensation is brief. Even with these difficulties, I want to make love to my beautiful wife. Because I am unable to help with the requisite action, making love is now another "chore" for Darlene who must pleasure both of us. Without an active participant who can return kisses and caresses, the intimacy is reduced. Also, I am not the most attractive person to look at anymore, with a tube connected to my neck and drool coming out of my mouth. Often during our occasional morning rendezvous, I interrupt the proceedings with a gurgle in my tracheotomy tube necessitating a tracheal suction. Intimacy and romance are lost to us. Yet I cling to what was because this is the only physical pleasure remaining for me and I still feel an intimate connection to Darlene through making love. Fortunately, Darlene still feels this connection to me and despite the changes we have had to make, I still see love in her eyes.

I miss fatherhood. I have not been able to enjoy my boys (and them me) through their teenage years as the active father I had envisioned myself being. No lazy golf afternoons, laughing at each other when one of us sliced the ball into the woods, no family ski trips, carving the hills with our snowboards, and no friendly games of two on two on our front driveway. I would have enjoyed these times as I enjoyed their childhoods.

I miss my calling. Most people define themselves to some extent by their occupation, and this is more so when you belong to a profession that the culture holds in esteem. As a physician, the title "Doctor" follows you not only at work but in every aspect of your life. I was proud to be a doctor, I enjoyed my work, I was proud of the things I did as a physician, and, most important, I was able to care for a great many people. My self-worth was wrapped up in my ability to help others. I could never imagine myself retiring from being a physician. Now I go to the doctor's office and I hear, "Mr. Sutherland, we are ready for you." They don't appreciate how this grates on me. *I am a doctor, goddamn it, just like you,* I want to say but do not. Of course, I can still care for people now and I do, but my impact is smaller. In my old life as a physician, I did not treat my patients, I cared for them genuinely. They were part of my family and I was honored that they chose me to help them. The provision of care gives us the feel-good endorphins and allows us a glimpse of our interconnectedness. Being needed gave me purpose.

I miss looking into people's eyes when I talk to them. I believe that you can see a person's soul by actively looking into his or her eyes when communicating. Eyes emote happiness, sadness, weariness, and peace. Now I use my eyes to talk, which is a technological miracle, but this requires me to have a screen in front of my face. I long for the soul-to-soul talks I used to have.

I miss walks. Walks at a slow pace, walks at a fast pace—also known as running—were a big part of me. When I was young my speed gave me confidence whether it was on the soccer pitch, a hiking trail, or football field. When I reached adulthood, leisurely strides, hand in hand with my partner, through parks and gardens, were pure bliss. In the middle of my career, the run down the back hallway to enter the birthing suite was a mixture of excitement, adrenaline, and fear of the unknown. At the end of my ability, I was running with my wife, and trying to keep up with the interests and activities of my children. I miss being physically fit and the freedom of going for a run. I took pride in being in good shape. Physical pleasures are all around us and generally the healthy take them for granted, as I did before ALS.

I miss tending my garden, by which I mean all the activities I would do around my home. In my free time, before the disease, I had enjoyed the creativity of gardening. The upkeep of living things, pruning away the dead and allowing new life to flourish, gave me peace. Home projects allowed me to stamp our house with my thoughts and feelings. Cooking enabled me to nourish my family and friends with food and love.

I miss smelling. Since my lungs are unable to move without the help of my tracheostomy and ventilator, I can no longer smell. I still have the senses to smell but the nerve endings are never stimulated because I breathe through my neck. The aromas of a freshly baked loaf of bread, newly mowed grass, and the lilacs in my yard are only memories. Of course, there are some advantages of not smelling, especially when I am around my sometimes gaseous sons.

I miss being musical. Whether you tap along to songs, play an instrument, or sing, you are allowed to express yourself in a manner that ultimately brings you peace and happiness. I loved to sing, perhaps more than people loved to hear me. My wife, children, friends, and drunken patrons at the local karaoke bar were the recipients of my "gift." Singing allowed me to express my love for the world. My son Nathaniel is a skilled guitarist. I am sure that if I was healthy, we would be able to sing and play together and it would be a shared passion between us.

I miss my independence. Before ALS, I was fiercely independent, seldom asking for help, always trying to figure out my own problems. Now my life is dependent upon others for every activity, from getting up in the morning to urinating. I cannot be left alone for fear that a mucus plug will block my airway. Independence is a trait that nurtures determination and patience. Fortunately, these qualities have helped me to live while being dependent.

Most of all, I miss my personhood. Being unable to speak or look people in the eye, I am often assumed to have lost my intelligence and other senses. I am generally ignored when out in public. If I take my family to dinner, wait staff tend to ignore me, even if I'm paying the bill. Darlene is often asked by old acquaintances, including some health-care professionals, "Can he hear me?" Or "Does he remember me?" These questions are directed at Darlene as though she were my interpreter, and even when I type out answers to their questions, using their first names, and my device replies to them, they continue to go through Darlene as if I am not there.

I knew I had lost my personhood two years after I had stopped my clinical practice. I was walking with Darlene (actually Darlene was driving me in my power wheelchair) on a path close to our house and we encountered a former patient of mine. I had known this man for about fifteen years and had taken care of his family through some difficult times. He saw me coming yet when we crossed paths all I got was a downward gaze. Not a word, not a quiet nod of recognition.

Another time, after my respiratory arrest, I was admitted to our regional hospital where I was treated as though I were unconscious. As an associate chief of staff for five years at two of the three hospitals in our health-care system, I knew a lot of the attending physicians from our monthly medical advisory committee meetings yet as a nonverbal patient under their care they no longer recognized me as a physician, or as a person. In general, some of my physician colleagues have shown the least empathy and compassion to me. Although some continue to support my cause through financial donations to the Walk for ALS, I miss the relationships. I have come to believe that I am their nightmare: a physician who has changed teams and become a patient.

This, to me, is the ultimate loss, when I fail to be recognized as the person I still am. My personality has not changed because of this disease. I am still kind, loving, conscientious, and I crave new achievements. I still have a sense of humor and am sensitive to self-perceived criticism. If I was not the same person I have always been, I would not be able to cope with my illness. It is hard to find peace with people who treat me otherwise.

* * *

None of this is to suggest that I spend all my time thinking about what I can no longer do. I was, and still am, reasonably content with the life Darlene and I have built, or rebuilt, for ourselves. I mention the things I missed and still miss, to help others gain perspective on the real pleasures of life. Personally, I am at least as conscious of the positives as of the negatives that have come with the changes in our lives. I am astonished that every setback, no matter how horrific, can have good in it.

Before I was diagnosed with ALS, I was probably working seventy hours a week between my clinic, the emergency room, obstetrics, inpatient, and administrative work. I managed to stay involved in my boys' activities, coaching whenever I had the skill to add something to their teams, and otherwise being an ardent spectator along with Darlene. But when ALS prevented me from working, I was home every afternoon as the boys arrived from school. I was ready and willing to talk with them, help them, or just be on the sideline as they did normal teenager stuff. Sharing these moments and knowing that I was available at a minute's notice when my family needed me was an opportunity ALS gave me.

I began to write letters to my family, including the birth stories mentioned previously, and more on birthdays and at Christmas. The idea was to leave something for my family to have when I was no longer there. The letters would include memories and, for the boys, my perspectives on how they had grown in the year and some advice on how they might make the most of themselves in the future. Mostly these letters were vehicles in which I could express my unconditional love to the boys and Darlene. They helped ensure that in our family appreciation and love were never left unsaid. Although that was the case before ALS, my illness brought it to a deeper and more urgent place.

A new activity brought into my life by my disease was fund-raising for a cause. A caring patient of mine organized a Walk for ALS in Georgetown, Ontario, and it has been continued annually through the efforts of family and friends. I've been overwhelmed by the support of my community and my friends at the Kinsmen club. We have brought in more money than almost any other part of Canada on a per-population basis. Like the late, Scott Ross Murray, Eddy Lefrançois and Tim Robertson, three others afflicted with ALS, I have become a Canadian champion of the cause.

While I mentioned earlier that my illness has been hard on some of my relationships, it also brought me closer to some old friends, including my first friend, John, who was a huge influence on me up until our high school years. After losing touch for twenty years, he has made a point of attending my Walks for ALS and stopping by to visit when he is in Toronto. A number of grade school friends stay in touch with e-mails and visits. My medical school friends visit every year for the ALS walk and, together with their wives, we have frequent reunions. The women from my old office still come by and we have wonderful and meaningful conversations. Friends that I have made in Georgetown would drop anything to help us. A few of the guys gather with me weekly to drink beer (them, not me) and watch sports on TV. One of my friends has learned how to take care of my suctioning needs, giving Darlene an evening's respite during my night with the guys. Others visit and sometimes cook for us. Another has written stories with me, and still another new friend keeps me up on everything he does, making it clear that I am doing him a favor by calling him for help. This is by no means a complete list of people who have played crucial roles at different times in my illness. I expect that they have gotten as much from me as I have gotten from them because that is how friendships work.

My younger brother, Brent, and his wife, Diane, made time with us a priority. Although his work is always busy, and my nephews have hectic schedules of their own, Brent takes the red-eye back and forth between Vancouver and Toronto to see us. We have become true friends as well as family. I know that each of our lives is richer for this relationship made stronger by my disease. My parents and Darlene's parents, too, love and support us. Like many other relationships, these have had their challenges but they have withstood the pressures of major illness and I am most grateful for them.

Yet another new role to enter my life was that of an advocate. As a physician, a terminal patient, and someone who wants to keep living despite glaring deficiencies, I am well positioned to speak for the right of others to determine their own tolerances for living with intractable diseases. I was given the opportunity to publish an editorial in a journal of my former peers at a time when medical aid in dying was becoming a reality in Canada. ALS is one of the diseases frequently raised when people discuss the merits of a planned death. I noted that I had the luxury of fighting my illness at a young age, with family and community support, and without financial pressure, and that not a lot of others enjoy the same circumstances. They are faced with a degenerative disease or terminal diagnosis and do not want their families to endure the hardships associated with a drawn-out death. I argued that we should respect their ability to make their own decisions regarding life or death. You will see that the term for medically assisted death has changed significantly in three years, from "physician-assisted suicide" to the now commonly used acronym MAID (medical assistance in dying). Here is an excerpt from my letter:

> I applaud the Supreme Court of Canada in its decision to strike down the ban of physician-assisted suicide. It is now time for physicians to provide leadership to develop protocols that enable physician-assisted suicide to become a reality in Canada. The need to protect the physician who is morally against this has to be acknowledged and legitimized. The protection of those not mentally capable has to be part of any protocols developed.
>
> I do not see this decision as delegitimizing my choice to live. I have been with families through births and deaths. I like to think my involvement in palliative care has helped ease the suffering of my patients. I don't know if I were still practicing medicine if I would be able to participate in a physician-assisted death, but when I was active and healthy I would not have thought I could live within the confines in which I currently do. Positions change with experiences. The Hippocratic Oath that physicians recite upon graduation tells us to do no harm to our patients. I think sometimes that our inaction with patients suffering with terminal illnesses does harm. Should my circum-stances change, I find comfort in the fact that I can now choose a gentle and humane death surrounded by loved ones on my own terms.

One of my largest accomplishments has been co-authoring a chil-dren's book about bullying. A friend of mine, Mike Parkhill, is passionate about preserving Indigenous languages, which he does mainly through the development of educational materials written in First Nations languages. He graciously gave me the opportunity to help him write the English version of a book to combat bullying. *Just Call Me Lucille* has been translated into numerous Indigenous languages and is a national bestseller. This feat improved my sense of self-worth.

Even in my weakened physical state, I think I can still educate and inspire people. Family, friends, and people with whom I correspond—those who are able to look beyond my machines and recognize that an intelligent, thoughtful, and loving person resides behind the screen—recognize that strength of spirit is much stronger than any physical state of being.

CHAPTER EIGHT

"You Have to Buy That House"

D ARLENE HAD BEEN TO A nearby restaurant to celebrate a friend's fiftieth birthday just before the long weekend in May 2015 when she noticed a property for sale. It was an attractive bungalow nestled among enormous trees along the Credit River in the village of Terra Cotta. She mentioned the house to me two days later, not really thinking that a move was in our future, although we knew that some change was required in our living arrangements. I had been home with my ventilator for nine months without any problems but we needed more adult space for our now grown sons. That very week we had replaced our furnace and had a draftsman come in to measure for a potential addition over the garage of our house.

After Darlene mentioned the listing, I looked it up online. I liked what I saw and thought it might be worthwhile for Darlene to check it out. Nathaniel and Zach were both home so I suggested Darlene take Zach with her. Zach had grown into a responsible young man and I trusted and valued his opinion on practically everything. Especially after my respiratory arrest, I saw that he would become the new head of our family should anything happen to me. (In retrospect, I would see that he had already quietly assumed the role when circumstances warranted.) Nathaniel, in grade twelve at this point, in spring 2015, often helped me out when Darlene was running errands. Nathaniel was our only son at home full-time since my return from the ICU with the ventilator. Ben and Zach were at college and university. Nathaniel had become greatly familiar with trach suctioning.

Zach went with Darlene to see the house. He took in the babble of the river, the mature trees stretching into the blue sky, the privacy of the setting, and said to his mother as they were leaving, "You and Dad have to buy that house." Ben, who was doing a construction engineering co-op placement, had been in our house that morning helping our draftsman friend with the measurements for an addition. He returned that evening to be told that Darlene and Zach were excited about moving to a different home. He was bewildered but soon shared in the excitement.

The next day we all went to see the new place together with our contractor and the draftsman who would examine the house for potential modifications necessary to accommodate a wheelchair. The existing configuration made for an extremely tight fit for my wheelchair on entering the kitchen. The bedrooms and the bathroom would have to be made accessible, and we saw an opportunity to bring more light and views of the river into the house. With these alterations, the property would have a natural, cottage-like feeling to it, a wonderful benefit given that our days of travel were behind us, while still keeping us just minutes away from our support network. We liked that it was all on one level, so no more elevators to contend with. The boys would have their own space in the basement, complete with their own kitchen, and they began making plans to turn the garage into a man cave for themselves and their friends. All of us loved the property. It was an attractive opportunity. We bought it.

We all pitched in to get the home in which we had lived for sixteen years on the market, with Zach doing the largest and most important chores. My job was to help Darlene design what we wanted in our new home. This project came at the perfect time for me. I needed something to make me excited about living again. It brought joy back into my life. With the help of our draftsman and our contractors, we did a complete renovation of the main floor, which led, inevitably, to a complete renovation of the basement. The scope of the project escalated, as happens with most projects, but we were happy to let it do so. It was a new beginning for our family.

We took possession of our new home in early September. The boys had enjoyed staying there even while it was under construction. Zach's long-term partner, Kaya, and her family gave us two kayaks which the boys loaded into our van and drove a few minutes upstream. They put the kayaks into the slow, narrow, shallow river and paddled home. They enjoyed the peace and tranquility that the river offered and were always popping in for a paddle.

Although Zach was now away at university, he came home frequently that fall to work on his pet project, the man cave, and to help us pack up the old house. Over Canadian Thanksgiving in October we moved all of our patio, shed, and garage contents to the new home. On Friday, November 13, we all moved into the barely completed house, its floors still covered with plywood to protect the new flooring underneath from the wear and tear of construction. Darlene occupied the new master bedroom and I took the new second bedroom. Nathaniel, Zach, Darlene, her mother, Phyllis, and several friends spent the rest of the weekend transferring our possessions from the old home to the new. We naively thought we had everything under control and told Ben to stay at school. We could have used him. The move that had started Friday did not finish until late Sunday. Nathaniel was the last one out of the old house. He wandered through its empty rooms, filming it all for posterity.

It was another five weeks before we had something approximating a kitchen and the boys were able to make a Christmas feast. After dinner I gave the family my 2015 Christmas note: *Much to my surprise 2015 has been a year of great change for all of us,* I wrote. *Change can be done for need or for opportunity. Thankfully this change has been done for the opportunity of a new beginning at a different stage of our lives.* I spoke of our new home, and how it represented to me an opportunity for Darlene and me to spend more of our time together as our sons embarked on their adult lives. I hoped the boys would know they always had a home and some independent space within as they worked toward establishing themselves in the larger world. There were special messages for each of our sons, congratulating them on the ways in which they had grown during the year, and another of my love and appreciation for Darlene. I acknowledged that despite our best intentions the Christmas tree and the house would scarcely be decorated for the season. We had been busy. *Thank you all for giving me a purpose and the love to carry on this journey called life,* I concluded. *Merry Christmas!*

CHAPTER NINE

February 21, 2016

U NSPEAKABLE HORROR CAN HIJACK your life at any time. For me, it has come during times I am most happy. We had just celebrated Darlene's fiftieth birthday with a wonderful party. I wrote a letter to her for this special occasion outlining fifty reasons why I love her. We were happy during this time despite the ALS. We had found a rhythm to our new life.

On Sunday, February 21, 2016, Nathaniel and his girlfriend, Erica, were traveling through the North Island of New Zealand. Ben was home from college for the weekend. Zach had just returned from a trip to Cuba. He had gone with friends from university in celebration of their graduation, which was close at hand. The highlight of the trip for him had been a side trip to a town off the tourist map where he had spoken to Cubans about their lives. He was impressed by how happy they were despite their lack of material wealth and came away convinced that North American life was a rat race in which we work continuously simply to support our consumerism. We debated with him the need for balance in all ideology.

Zach and Ben went for a short paddle, the usual route, putting in upstream about forty-five minutes by water from our house. It was a leisurely ride on the calm river, surrounded by nature, and they arrived home close to dusk. Zach's girlfriend, Kaya, was there to greet them and help with the car retrieval. Kaya and Zach enjoyed the evening together in his room.

The next morning, after my exercises, I went to the kitchen and caught a glimpse of Zach and Kaya on the deck embracing each other and looking out at the river. They were in T-shirts basking in the sunshine on an unseasonably warm (fifteen degrees Celsius) day. Later we had a great talk with them as Zach prepared their breakfast. Zach had been devouring cooking shows and was demonstrating how to cook scrambled eggs in a pot, the Jamie Oliver method. As with every new dish he made a point of showing me the finished product—in this case, fluffy scrambled eggs. We talked about future plans, with the Eagles song "Peaceful Easy Feeling" playing in the background.

They had about an hour before Zach had to return to university and decided to take advantage of the warm February day and retrace the kayak route that Ben and Zach had traveled the evening before. I heard a squeal from Kaya as she put on the hip waders. There was a little ice in the boot from the night before.

I was looking through pictures that Nathaniel had sent me from New Zealand and Darlene was on the phone with her parents when we noticed that Zach and Kaya had been out for more than an hour. Not thinking much about it, we sent Ben to see where they were. Ben did the one-minute drive and saw the kayaks, empty, on one of the two iced areas of the river. Not seeing Zach or Kaya anywhere, he returned and told us to call 911 and went out again looking for them. We contacted Kaya's parents who quickly drove down the hill into Terra Cotta to be confronted by the terrifying sight of rescue-vehicle lights.

When Ben first came to tell us of the empty kayaks, I could not imagine anything worse than a dump into the cold, knee-high water that prevails along most of the river. As the minutes and then hours ticked on, I helplessly waited for any word of what was going on just a few hundred yards from where I sat in my wheelchair. My friend Mike was by my side, as was my friend James who had come over for a friendly visit and unwittingly walked into every parent's nightmare: not knowing what has happened to your child.

As we waited, I did all I was able to: pray for the safety of Zach and Kaya. I knew after an hour that my prayers would go unanswered, but it would take two and a half hours before I knew the truth. During this time, Darlene, Ben, our friend Jennifer, and Kaya's family would have to witness the finding of the lifeless shell in which Kaya had once lived. Zach was nowhere to be found. I remember Jennifer and Duncan Firth coming into our house to retrieve Kaya's overnight bag. In Jennifer's shocked, haunted expression of absolute loss, I recognized all the emotion that my body was unable to display.

CHAPTER TEN

Memorials

I HAD ALWAYS FELT I would innately sense when my loved ones were in danger. I had sensed nothing when this tragedy happened. I had had no ability to sense Zach's physical death. This made me question my spiritual connection with him. Days later, Nathaniel shared with us a dream he had on the other side of the world at exactly the time of the accident: Zach and Kaya were in the water and they were in trouble.

The day ended with Darlene having to make the calls to tell close family that "there has been an accident." We knew Kaya had passed but Zach's body had not been found. The hardest call was to Nathaniel and his girlfriend who were five weeks into a five-month adventure. My brother Brent, who just three weeks earlier at our home had enjoyed some special one-on-one time with Zach, dropped everything to join us. My parents arranged for a flight and Darlene's parents got in their car and made the twenty-two-hour drive from Nova Scotia to Ontario. Wei, my friend and family physician, spent a few days between us and the Firth family home, just to be present and to assist wherever he could.

Our grieving could not start until Zach was found. Helicopters equipped with sonar devices flew back and forth over our home trying to locate his remains. The sound of low-flying helicopters continues to be a trigger forever linking us to this time. The next day, February 22, they concentrated their search on the thick ice where the kayaks were found. Searchers carefully cut away block after block of ice while a crowd of neighbors, friends, and even my estranged brother held vigil with the hope that Zach would be discovered. Around midmorning, February 23, his body was located at the end of our property across the river. Close to where he was found, a set of stairs from forgotten times ascended to nowhere. The two-day wait for this resolution gave us a profound appreciation for the feelings of hope and unresolved grief that torment families who never find their lost beloved.

A mute, shocked Nathaniel arrived home Tuesday evening through the great assistance of Erica. Ben took him down to the basement and somehow brought him to a place where he could talk again. Our best friends, Craig and Carol, and their sons came to be with us. Friends bombarded our house with kindness and love. Neighbors dropped off food, which was appreciated, although at this time we had little appetite. Darlene and I, from time to time, retreated to the bedroom with the boys to get away from everyone trying to help.

Together with the Firth family, we talked openly about our shared loss of two great children. This was the start of an incredibly supportive relationship forged by the love of our children. Our local newspaper gave us the opportunity to write tributes to Zach and Kaya. We wrote about the love they gave to us and others. With so many out-of-town friends and family members present or arriving, we hastily prepared a memorial for Zach just four days after he was found.

My Kinsmen friend who is a funeral director came to our home and helped with the funeral arrangements. Because Zach's body had undergone an autopsy after being in the water for two days, we decided to have it cremated. He advised us not to see the body so that our last vision of Zach would remain the handsome and strong young man we saw leaving the house that Sunday afternoon. Ben and Nathaniel carefully chose items that Zach had loved to accompany his body and to dwell forever in his ashes: these included the Blue Jays hat that was forever on his head, his all-purpose chinos, his long-sleeved striped shirt, his Cole Haan shoes, photos of happy family times and numerous other personal mementos.

We decided as a family to have a private memorial but made sure to include any of Zach's friends who wanted to attend. We did not want the occasion open because we did not have the strength to see everyone whom Zach had touched in his short lifetime. Our priest supported our choice of a nonreligious memorial. It was important to us that we be authentic to Zach. Two days before the memorial, Ben, Nathaniel, Darlene, and I sequestered ourselves in the master bedroom and talked about who we would ask to attend, concentrating on people who had been important in Zach's life.

We talked about my estranged brother and his family attending. Nathaniel and Ben were initially against their participation. In the boys' eyes, my brother and his family had chosen not to be a part of Zach's life for the previous six years. I knew they would have to attend for the support of my parents and because they were a very important part of the first fourteen years of Zach's life. We reached a compromise in that my brother would be invited but with the condition that the families keep their distance during this extremely vulnerable time. The decision to have them attend with conditions was never about shaming. It was all we could give to them in that moment.

The memorial was held at the golf club where Zach had worked for two summers and our friends were invaluable in taking care of arrangements and catering details. Craig helped us structure the memorial. I took charge of the music, choosing a soundtrack that Zach would have found deep with meaning. I also prepared notes for our priest to use as Darlene stayed up late writing about Zach and Kaya's relationship from kindergarten onward. Nathaniel was invaluable to his mom with the computer problems she encountered because of a brain not functional due to shock. Carol and Darlene's mother gathered up photographs of Zach, Kaya, and our family to illustrate the story of our love. The collages from our families gave everyone a reminder of the life that Zach had lived, strong and active, his smile always present and his eyes emitting kindness.

On a blue-sky day, we formally said goodbye to Zach's physical embodiment. The memorial was full of people from our past and present, including my oldest friends from Halifax and medical school friends. Carol read Darlene's beautiful tribute to Zach and Kaya. Craig and Carol's son Mackenzie read the lyrics to a song by Rush called "Afterimage," and Brent read some of the letters that I, believing that my own death was close at hand, had been writing as a legacy to our boys. My family sat in the front row, across from the Firth family. Both of Zach's grandfathers and his closest friends shared their favorite stories about him. They were all beautiful and full of the essence of Zach.

On Tuesday, we formally said goodbye to Kaya, another memorial full of love for a beautiful person. Darlene and I cried more during Kaya's service than Zach's, probably because we were able to be more unguarded and our new reality had crept in. There were also two vigils held for Zach and Kaya in the village of Terra Cotta. Over four hundred people mourned the tragic loss that had occurred just six days earlier, shattering the innocence of the river. We did not have the strength to attend these vigils but are forever grateful to our new community for honoring the lives of Zach and Kaya. The Sutherland and Firth families expressed our thanks in a letter to *The Independent and Free Press* (Georgetown and Acton):

The outpouring of support from the . . . community is beyond what words could truly express. We appreciate that it has been done so respectfully, without any expectations from anyone who has been so kind as to drop off food, send a card, write a letter, put a flag at half-mast, or arrange a vigil during this unfathomable loss of two incredibly beautiful people, Kaya and Zach. Family and close friends meant absolutely everything to Kaya and Zach. They adored their brothers, Jackson, Isaac, Ben, and Nathaniel. Their bonds went beyond being siblings—they were also one another's best friends.

The number of family and friends who dropped everything upon hearing the unthinkable news and immediately started driving, or hopped on the earliest plane, from literally everywhere around the world in our time of need is beyond comprehension. That is what love is and demonstrates what happens when you surround yourselves with amazing friends and family members who have chosen to support your values.

People have said to all of us as parents, "you are so strong." We are all far from strong. We are broken beyond belief, but we remain parents to four incredible young men and for us not to be there to help them heal and achieve their dreams would result in each family losing all of its children to this horrific nightmare. We know that would not be honoring Zach and Kaya. As we begin to move forward, we are all terrified as our unimaginable loss becomes a reality.

The tragic accident will remain just that—a situation, on a beautiful spring-like day, that suddenly shifted. Unfortunately, all the things that could have gone wrong at that precise moment in time were never considerations [for Zach and Kaya]. They felt safe in nature. They were excited to share a quiet hour together kayaking before they headed back to university.

As we start our grieving process, one of the most precious gifts that everyone can give our families to help us heal is to take some time to write about an experience or simple interaction that involved either Kaya or Zach or them as a couple. Please send it to our families through either the mail or in care of Jones Funeral Home. These memories will give us comfort in the days, months, and years ahead.

Zach and Kaya were all about making the world a better place and always brought happiness to those around them. They had no tolerance for meanness or exclusion and never surrounded themselves with negative energy. If you see our families or close friends around town, please just smile and allow us our space. Please appreciate that we know you care without words being exchanged. We are all hurting and very vulnerable right now. We are not being rude.

We know that Kaya and Zach touched many lives, both young and old, in their short twenty-one years on earth. We know so many people are hurting and remain in disbelief. We are encouraging everyone to seek professional support if they are not sure how to process this sudden, senseless loss. Unfortunately, the answer to our question—"Why?"—will remain unanswered in our lifetime.

CHAPTER ELEVEN

The Abyss

MANY PEOPLE HAVE TURNING points in their lives that present them with a new and lesser reality in which they must gather strength and try to move forward. In the decade after my diagnosis of ALS, my immediate family had learned to accept the bad news and rise to the challenge of remaking our world, and we had managed to find a new normal despite my limitations. I was consoled by the notion that things could not get much worse. I had taken the bullet of misfortune for my family—my life was the sacrifice that would ensure that the rest of them would be spared further tragedy. We had got through it and we were even able to find some happiness amid all the loss, particularly in our house by the river, which all of us were excited about and viewed as a new beginning. Zach, who was just finishing his degree and was about to embark on his future, had been most excited of all.

And then, out of the blue, we were kicked down again into life's deepest depths. I had thought that facing my illness and its inevitable ending was tough but it did not prepare me for the magnitude of this loss. Zach and Kaya were taken from us in a freak accident that happened, like most accidents, on a beautiful day, and, also like most accidents, less than five minutes from home. Unfortunately, some families and individuals get more than their fair share of defining moments.

During the official ceremonies for the remembrances of Zach and Kaya we were numb and in shock. Our only concern at the time was remaining authentic to Zach and supporting one another in our shattered nuclear family of myself, Darlene, Ben, and Nathaniel. I had naively thought this was also the goal of my parents, but two days after Zach's memorial I received an e-mail from my father expressing disappointment that the whole of our family had not been able to grieve together. The real message in this was he was frustrated that my older brother and his family were not given the privilege of being with the rest of the family.

At the memorial, my mother and father had decided to not sit with my family. I interpreted this, rightly or wrongly, as a protest of our not forgiving my older brother for his six years of indifference to the well-being of my family. The e-mail destroyed me and yet again showed me that gigantic loss was followed by more loss. In addition to the death of my oldest son, I faced a wrenching disruption in my relationship with my parents. Once again, I felt as though I was to blame for everything that had transpired among my family, my brother's family, and my parents over the last six years. I met my father's e-mail with a forceful reply. My older brother, copied on my response, was captured by my anger and probably did not deserve it as he had done everything that I had asked of him during the memorial without complaint.

Having been a peacemaker all my life, I next suggested to my parents that a face-to-face discussion between them, myself, and Darlene should follow so that we could put some of this unpleasantness behind us. The meeting occurred two days later and in retrospect we probably should have waited longer until some of our anger had dissipated. The loss of Zach just threw gasoline on the embers of perceived slights that had been felt long ago and almost forgotten. Now they were roaring fires. People don't always behave empathetically after sudden loss. Minds, numbed with the shock of tragedy, sometimes can't comprehend the results of their actions on those at the center of the tragedy. Their anger was that the family continued to be divided. Our anger was over how every good and terrible event in our lives was always measured by its effect on them. Nevertheless, these slights accumulated in all of our grieving minds. What was supposed to be a peacemaking discussion started volatile and ended with Mom stomping off to the car, saying to my son Ben that she had lost a son to ALS and now a grandson. That was hard on Ben, who had lost a brother and best friend in Zach, and who lived day to day with a father who had ALS and was still very much alive.

My dad did stay with us for an hour after Mom's departure to try to make peace out of a terrible situation. There was no way to remedy things, however. Just ten days after losing Zach and Kaya, I felt that I had also lost a close and meaningful relationship with my parents. The ramifications of an estranged family are intensely felt, especially in a moment when a family is supposed to come together. Everyone involved in that meeting lost something. I believe it is also accurate to say that I lost most.

Throughout this episode, I was conscious of my disease. I knew it was affecting my ability to grieve and to comfort others who were in grief. When you cannot move and share hugs, when you cannot communicate in your own voice with the right emotional tone, when you are always two minutes behind the conversation because of the time it takes to spell out each word on a screen, you are at a significant disadvantage. Disagreements can occur and gather force before you are able to react. You do not have the agility to navigate away from problems. You can't alleviate your own grief with physical distractions like a long run, or by finding the bottom of a bottle. A feeling of helplessness is normal in the face of loss. Mine was profound.

The first reaction of anyone after a personal tragedy is to curl up in a ball and retreat from life's insults. In the aftermath of the memorials, Darlene had to force herself to eat as she was essentially doing ninety percent of my daytime care. She was so consumed with grief she was sure that she was going crazy. At the end of the first week, we got professional help from a psychologist who kindly made a house call. During our first session, I remember Ben saying, "I can't possibly lose my Dad now, too!" This statement, on all of our minds, shouted how fragile my life now appeared after the loss of our strong and vibrant son and brother, and Kaya. We met with the psychologist two or three times in the weeks that followed. She helped assure each of us that we were not going crazy: we were all in shock and operating in our primitive minds where the rules of fight, flight, or freeze prevailed. This in itself was valuable knowledge to assist in our early survival. Darlene and I also started meeting twice a week with Kaya's parents, Duncan and Jennifer, sharing our feelings with the only other people who could truly understand the immensity of our grief.

I felt keenly and immediately the loss of happiness I derived from seeing my boys grow and reach their milestones. I still had this for Ben and Nathaniel but knew that each milestone they reached would remind us of those denied Zach and that their lives would always be more of a struggle without their older brother beside them. Eventually, they would have to cope with my loss, also. What eight years ago was a family of five without a care in the world would become a family of three able people with two significant holes that could only be partially filled with new relationships and love.

While I knew that we were not the only family facing devastating losses, I could not help but think of the many who had been spared significant tragedy. I did not have to look far to find families who had not lived what a reasonable person would consider caring and compassionate lives yet appeared not to have encountered major setbacks. I knew from previous experience that jealousy and envy were negative emotions that would only stand in the way of my healing and my coming to terms with my losses, and I knew that I should not judge, but being human I could not help it. Nor could I keep myself from thinking ahead to more loss, to the inevitability of family and friends being unable to deal with the enormity of our suffering and withdrawing from our lives. I could tell myself that we had dealt with ALS and found a sense of normality even after it had done its worst but I had no idea how, after Zach's death, we would ever be able to find joyous participation in life again.

One unexpected development in the weeks after our loss came courtesy of Courtney, a daughter of some close friends. She was linked to this disaster on two fronts. She had known Zach her entire life, and she had been part of the Firth family through a long-term relationship with Kaya's youngest brother. During a trip to Florida a few weeks after the accident, her great-aunt told her that she had found comfort during some of her own losses by consulting spiritual mediums. Through the years and a process of trial and error, she had found one in whom she had developed real trust. Courtney arranged for an over-the-phone reading with her great-aunt's medium. She had a consoling interaction with him. She said that she was certain she had been communicating with Kaya.

Courtney's mother told us of this experience and gave us the medium's contact information in case we might find comfort in this sort of consultation. Before the loss of Zach and Kaya, we had no need to consult spiritual mediums, and nothing in our scientific training had prepared us to be open to experiences of this nature. We wondered how mediums could make contact with the spirits, and especially how they did it over the telephone. We thought about it and discussed it with Ben and Nathaniel and decided to arrange a telephone call. It is accurate to say that we wanted to believe we would be in touch with Zach. We were closed-minded and skeptical on the one hand, sad and desperate on the other. During the forty-minute reading, we answered yes and no to a variety of questions, afraid of giving away too much information. Even in our closed-minded state, we noticed that the medium was able to bring forth information that only we and Zach knew. The messages were full of love and appreciation for a life well-lived. We knew that this was Zach and our feelings of loss were alleviated just a little as we began this new relationship with Zach "in spirit."

CHAPTER TWELVE

At Five Weeks

(In the months after our tragedy, I kept notes on our grief. They are presented here as I recorded them.)

F IVE WEEKS HAVE PASSED, one for every member of our little family, and the forever of our loss is settling on us. The anguish and sorrow are etched in Darlene's face. She's convinced that no happiness can exist in our future. "If I didn't have the boys, I would die," she says. *And I am only living for you*, I think.

It's a terrible morning. Darlene awakens to find I've soiled myself; then when I'm put on the commode there is another mess. More shit that my wife has to deal with on top of Easter without Zach. It is a day of absolutes for Darlene: "We never will be happy," and, "We will always carry this." I begin questioning anew whether my existence is helping or harming her long-term happiness.

It was at times like these that Zach could be counted on to wrap his arms around Darlene in a tight embrace and say convincingly, "Everything will be okay, Mom." From the time I was diagnosed, Zach had known that our family's healing required him to lead by example. With his smile and joyful laugh, he would be first to face reality and keep everyone moving forward. Now we're missing his

presence greatly. We have only his remains, brought to us on Easter
Sunday by some good friends. Zach's ashes are in a handcrafted box;
Kaya's grandfather has made one for each of them. Ben has skill-
fully etched on this the symbols of Zach's beloved sports teams, an
infinity loop with his and Kaya's initials, and a sketch of the maple
tree standing tall outside our kitchen. Since moving here we have
named this tree the Tree of Life. Fortunately, Nathaniel comes into
the bedroom as if summoned by Zach and gives his mother the hug
she so desperately needs, the hug I would give her if I could. Grief
is even lonelier for Darlene without a husband to hold, kiss, and
comfort her.

I sit long days staring at my screen with a blank look on my face.
Time to think was one of the luxuries of my disease but now it brings
constant reminders of the losses that have accumulated over the last
eight years. I think of that fateful telephone call to Darlene after my
diagnosis: "I need to tell you something." And our subsequent conversation with the boys: "We need to tell you something important."
I dwelled on the senselessness of our most recent tragedy. Because
articulating an experience helps somehow to manage it, I look up the
definition of tragedy on my screen: "an event causing great suffering,
destruction, or distress." It definitely fits.

* * *

Two weeks later, nothing much has changed. "I can't believe this
is happening to us," Darlene says, weeping, at the start of the day.
"We had enough with ALS." We are reading books about grief and
recovery in our quest to deal effectively with our situation. They all
present the same ideas. Everyone grieves in their own way and on
their own timeline. It is important to grieve (inward feelings) and to
mourn (the outward display of grief). I recognize that I have been
grieving but have limited my mourning when with Darlene, the

boys, and the Firths. I have been trying to appear strong to others, which gets in the way of me mourning properly. Like most men, I don't want to share my vulnerabilities with my friends.

I mistakenly click on a news article about the accident that took Zach and Kaya. As usual, there are trolls in the comments section: *February kayaking without life jackets or wet suits, what did you expect?* This, of course, suggests that they were reckless and somehow deserved to die. They were far from reckless to those who knew them. It was a warm afternoon. The river takes a slow, meandering course near our home. Ninety percent of it is only three feet deep. All the boys had been kayaking on it all winter, and the evening before Zach had traveled the exact same route with his brother. The two sections of ice were no problem for the boys. Zach was a lifeguard. Kaya had been kayaking in these same kayaks since she was three years old, on the lake where her family cottaged. The pair of them would have been more at risk driving to school than paddling down the river.

We know that they navigated the first patch of ice without incident. We know that the second section of ice, closer to our home, was perhaps caused by a tree that had fallen into the river, creating a deeper pool where the water slowed enough that ice formed during unseasonably cold weather the week before. A witness saw them standing safely on the first section of ice and thought there was nothing unusual or reckless about what he saw. We know nothing about what happened from that point on, except for the obvious. One got into trouble and the other tried to help. That was the type of young adults they were. One could not have stood by while the other was at risk. They were each other's soul mate. I write to the troll, "know all the facts of the story before you fucking judge."

One helpful thing in all our reading deals with guilt. As parents and the last people to see Zach and Kaya before the accident, we cannot help but think about all the things we might have done to ensure that what happened would not have happened. This brings guilt. If you look at the definition of guilt, it says that you need to intend harm to be guilty. No one close to this situation intended to do harm, especially not the victims themselves.

* * *

On the Sunday of the seventh week, I am listening to the radio for the first time since the day of the accident. I have been purposely avoiding this three-hour CBC Radio program because the day of the accident Kaya had been talking about an opportunity to be a panelist on the show. The seven weeks that I have waited have not been long enough and as we listen in the first hour to a discussion with a panel of university students about whether the university experience is educating students well, I think, *I should be hearing Kaya right now*.

The final hour of the broadcast features a documentary about Viktor Frankl, the concentration camp survivor and author of *Man's Search for Meaning*. His book deals with his tremendous losses of family and freedom during the Holocaust, and how he found meaning for his life despite his circumstances and, eventually, new happiness as well. It occurs to me that his thoughts might help me deal with the old realities of ALS and the grim new realities of the loss of two beloved individuals.

Not long after hearing that broadcast, I am able to listen to Zach's favorite radio program. He loved sports talk shows. I know that if he was still with us, they would have been part of his afternoon routines as he worked on his man cave or whatever else he was doing. I can see him calling in and arguing with the host. The show is talking this day about the Toronto Raptors and their playoff series with Indiana, which is tied two games apiece. The Raptors have been playing horribly and there is another crucial game tonight. I've been missing Zach's insights into how the Raptors and the Toronto Blue

Jays are doing, which I suppose is a mundane part of the experience of missing Zach.

I was never one to watch regular season sports games. I was too busy playing sports when younger, and there were no local professional teams in Atlantic Canada to build an allegiance to. As I got older, I was busy with work or the boys' activities. When ALS struck, I preferred to watch movies. It was Zach who brought us around to investing time in the Raptors. His enthusiasm was contagious. He did the same with the Blue Jays during baseball season. I would read up on the trades and drafts to keep pace with Zach's voluminous knowledge.

Darlene and I became closer to Zach through his teams. He knew how to play his mom when watching the Blue Jays in the 2015 American League Divisional series. After a disappointing inning, Darlene quickly lost faith and said the Jays were doomed. Zach managed to talk her into a one-sided bet in which she would pay him $100 if the Jays pulled out a victory. There were no consequences for him if they did not, so he could not lose. Sure enough, the Jays turned the game around and Darlene absorbed an expensive lesson in keeping faith and hope alive against the odds. On reflection, I think Zach deliberately, if not consciously, created a common interest among us, one that I could still enjoy despite my ALS. It is as though his spirit, knowing that he was predetermined to leave us early, left us something in which we could continue to feel his presence, a special bond with him. When I follow sports now, I feel him watching with me over my shoulder, as I share his faith and hope.

* * *

The excitement and hope that the spiritual medium readings initially produced has been replaced with the same old feelings of the loss of Zach and Kaya from our lives. This feeling of loss is punctuated with each basketball or baseball game we watch, each renovation we complete on this house that Zach brought us to, and with every step forward that Ben and Nathaniel take on their journey to wellness.

We are moving forward but some days we go back to the beginning. Healthy healing methods do not appear as an option for us when we are overwhelmed by the exhaustion of grief and the struggle of just making it through my daily care needs. Next Sunday will be Mother's Day, yet another holiday that underscores our new reality. I have no idea how we can celebrate without one piece of our family. Eventually, we will need to find a way but the sense of loss will continue to be part of every holiday and milestone. This summer Zach will officially graduate from university, an achievement I did not think I would live to see. My worst nightmare would not have conjured a world in which Zach would be the one missing. His honor will have to pass without our involvement because to witness everyone else celebrating their new beginnings would be too painful for us. It is something else that we will have to ignore while practically everyone else can enjoy the achievements of their children.

Mother's Day has always brought mixed emotions for Darlene. Early in my diagnosis, they tended to be about expectations not met. I could not do much to make the day special so it was on the boys to celebrate their mother. They did their best—making breakfast and leaving the dishes for Darlene to wash. It was unfair that the responsibility fell so heavily on them. The last two Mother's Days had been better. The boys made nice cards and bought flowers and cooked elaborate dinners. They even cleaned up after the meals! This year, Ben and Nathaniel made a wonderful brunch of Belgian waffles, omelets and fruit cocktail and gave Darlene a card. Ben had printed the boys' names on the card, in order: *Zach, Ben, Nathaniel.* Because Ben, like Zach, is left-handed, it was almost as though Zach had signed the card.

Jennifer came over and shared more treasures from Zach and Kaya, love notes from grade twelve when Kaya went on the annual school trip (i.e., party trip) to Cuba. We did not really want the boys to go on these unsupervised excursions so we made a rule that if they went, they paid. Only Nathaniel made the trip. Zach, like Ben, did not raise the funds, which turned out to be a blessing for me. While Kaya was away, Zach drove us to Boston so that I could participate in a brain-computer-interface experiment. We arrived in Boston on a sunny warm afternoon and two hours later a transformer blew up near our boutique hotel and the whole downtown was blacked out. The hotel was evacuated to the lobby—everyone except me and, by extension, my family—due to the elevators not working. The boys went to an unaffected hotel's lobby that night to charge a battery so that my BiPap would work, an example of the mature, caring sons we had raised. Fortunately, the electricity in the hotel was restored by around two thirty a.m. The only thing Zach had been looking forward to on the trip was a tour of Fenway Park. Due to our late start in the morning, the boys arrived just as the last tour was finishing. The notes that Jennifer brought over gave me a glimpse into what must have been in the back of his mind while all this was going on.

* * *

We have been searching for answers, reading books about the afterlife, souls, karma, and the earth as a learning classroom for experiences that will allow a soul to get closer to its creator. My readings persuade me that it is conceivable that everything is predestined and I could not have changed what has occurred. It does seem that both of their lives were wrapped up too conveniently as if on some level their souls had prepared for their otherwise untimely physical deaths.

I wonder about luck and Friday the thirteenth. We are thirteen weeks from the passing of Zach and Kaya. Darlene and I became a couple on a Friday the thirteenth, I wrote my wedding vows on a Friday the thirteenth, and we moved to our new house by the river on a Friday the thirteenth. We used to feel that Friday the thirteenths, unlucky for the rest of the world, were lucky days for us. Now we question our good fortune and whether it was moving here on that day that brought us tragedy just three (3) months and one (1) week later. I think it must be a natural human impulse to look for patterns, to reach for anything that seems to make sense of a senseless loss.

It is impossible to avoid the what-ifs. For instance, what if I had died on August 7, 2014? If I had perished instead of going on artificial life support, the family would not have moved to a house on the river thirteen months after my death, and Zach and Kaya would never have been on that river thirteen weeks ago. Would my death have saved their lives? It is a bargain I would gladly have made.

Who knows. Maybe I was kept here because Zach and Kaya were going to die, and I would be needed to help my family heal. Maybe this is my life lesson: not only to have suffered the loss of a working body but also to endure the psychological trauma of losing a child. I guess it comes down to beliefs. Belief in predestination, the idea that the exits of Zach and Kaya were orchestrated by the universe, or, on the contrary, belief that their physical deaths were simply a freak accident. Questions such as these will not be answered in this lifetime. If we keep faith that there is some type of grand design to both our physical and our nonphysical existence, it will lessen some of our sufferings.

CHAPTER THIRTEEN

At Fourteen Weeks

THIS WEEK I TURN FIFTY. Naturally, I compare my life at forty to my life at fifty. People's lives can vary greatly in this decade, of course, through divorce, illness, and work changes but my life at fifty is almost unrecognizable. Obviously, the fitness and strength that I had always treasured are gone. I am on life support with a feeding tube in my stomach and a breathing tube in my neck. My professional life is over, from the hands-on work of delivering babies and working in emergency rooms to the teaching of medical residents to my administrative responsibilities. My marriage has changed, with Darlene turning into a caregiver. And we have unexpectedly lost Zach and Kaya. It seems to me an inconceivable amount of change, and it is difficult for me, even though I have adapted to my circumstances, not to dwell on the losses. It occurs to me that I had never really taken the time to grieve my own disease. I was always too busy trying to make the lives of my family as normal as possible, enjoying our boys and their accomplishments while ignoring the elephant in the room, the fact that I had joined the severely disabled club and was on artificial life support.

It takes a letter from Darlene to remind me that I need to acknowledge the things I've lost and make peace with their disappearance from my life and rely upon the many things that remain to help me through the times when the losses seem overwhelming. From what I still have, she says, I will find meaning in my life.

I have been trying. In recent weeks, we sent Ben, his girlfriend Savannah, Nathaniel, and Erica to the Dominican Republic to lighten their moods and hopefully fan the embers of happiness in their hearts. We also thought that Nathaniel and Erica might need help facing airports and travel again after their last trip home. We knew that if they traveled with Ben and Savannah this first step would be easier. I've been reading a lot in the meantime, searching for comfort. I'm drawn to Neil Peart's lyrics in the Rush song "BU2B2," which I remember hearing with Zach and Nathaniel during the band's Clockwork Angels tour. Peart himself had experienced unfathomable loss, his daughter passing away in a car accident and his wife passing away of cancer less than a year later.

I was brought up to believe
Belief has failed me now
The bright glow of optimism
Abandoned me somehow

Belief has failed me now
Life goes from bad to worse
No philosophy consoles me
In a clockwork universe

Life goes from bad to worse
I still choose to live
Find a measure of love and laughter
And another measure to give

I still choose to live
And give, even while I grieve
Though the balance tilts against me
I was brought up to believe

I read Frankl's *Man's Search for Meaning*. There is great wisdom in its pages and I make a record of the quotes I find particularly meaningful:

A man with a why can survive any how.
The truth that love is the highest goal to which man can aspire.
The salvation of man is through love and to love.
Love goes far beyond the physical person of the beloved.

All of these speak to me and tell me that Zach and Kaya in their short lives did achieve the highest goal to which we can aspire, having found in each other an enduring love.

I also read about a physician's near-death experience. In *Proof of Heaven: A Neurosurgeon's Journey into the Afterlife*, Dr. Eben Alexander recounts being in a coma due to meningitis. He describes his encounter with heaven, an all-seeing and all-knowing God, with multiple universes, and with a spiritual world far vaster than the physical world. His message is that the spiritual world and unconditional love completely surround us. I am somewhat comforted by his belief in the continuation of life after death, and in the idea of a soul beyond the physical body, although I cannot help but ask why an all-knowing God who surrounds us with unconditional love would take Zach and Kaya.

* * *

On my birthday, Jennifer, Kaya's mother, was on the riverside at the edge of our property where Zach was ultimately found two days after the accident. While meditating, she had a vision of her daughter with Zach. Kaya was dressed in a white dress with spaghetti straps and had a single white flower in her hair. Zach was clean shaven like he had been when they left on their short kayak run. Each had a radiant smile. Zach made a gesture toward our house that she took as an instruction to spread the news to his family that they are happy. This message is one of the best birthday gifts I have received. Ben and Nathaniel also made me a wonderful card from themselves and Zach. Darlene wrote an incredible card (more an essay) to help raise my spirits, and my brother Brent came to give us emotional support. These are some of the things I have.

Most weeks since the accident we have spent at least five hours with Kaya's parents, Duncan and Jennifer. These sessions provide enormous comfort to all of us. Recently, they have become more about how we will shape our new lives. The boys in each family will be our focus for the immediate future. They need to be happy and looking toward their own futures. They need to live fulfilled lives without the physical presence of Zach and Kaya, yet knowing that the spirits of their brother and sister will be forever in their lives. The problem is that we all want so much more than that. We want more time with Zach and Kaya, here and now.

* * *

We hear of another person's spiritual reading in which Zach appears. Zach says that people are blaming him for the accident. He says that he was smart, that he "owns" the decision he made, and that he would do the exact same thing again under the same circumstances. This plays on my mind. I doubt that it was actually Zach speaking through the medium because previously he has given us to believe he is feeling more happiness than regret.

The reading is still on my mind a couple of days later when I receive an e-mail from a relative. She says that my article about medically assisted dying, which was carried on the front page of a national newspaper, had "interesting opinions" and that I should not only be an advocate for assistance in dying and ALS but also for water safety.

I write all this in a letter to Zach, telling him that the e-mail has thrown me and angered me, in part because his concerns, as expressed through the medium, were echoed in this judgment from a family member. I wait two days (double the usual rule for airing grievances) to decide if and how I will respond to the e-mail. In the meantime, I read about the topic of victim blame and discover that it is common for people to blame victims so as to distance themselves from the idea that anything similar could happen to them personally. Sometimes the more innocent the victim, the more likely this is to occur. I write to this relative:

Hello,

Likewise, I will be direct with you. Your statement in your last email really threw me.

When you suggest that I should be an advocate for water safety, it suggests to me that you blame Zach for his death.

The coroner deemed the deaths an accident, not a preventable accident, thus saying that life jackets would not have been an expectation for the given circumstances.

I think the only way it would have been prevented is by their simply not going, but given their experience in kayaks and the beautiful conditions of the day, the risk of them dying would be extremely low, similar to getting into a fatal motor vehicle accident on a rainy day.

Victim blame makes everyone else feel safe because "it couldn't happen to me because I wouldn't have. . ."

In Zach's and Kaya's situation, it does not honor their intellect and level of responsibility.

The river is not like you are used to. It is ninety percent three-feet deep and twenty-feet wide. There were two deaths only because one got into trouble and the other tried to save that person. That was how much they loved each other.

The water safety lesson would be to not teach your kids to be lifeguards because by doing that they might try to save someone's life.

Jeff

I got a reply that crushed me. Darlene saw me in distress and looked at my screen (I had been trying to shelter her from my family's craziness in the wake of the tragedy). The e-mail insisted in blaring capital letters that a person should not be on a river in mid-February. It is not safe because of the temperature of the water and I, as a doctor, should have known better than to let Zach go out in the kayak. In short, I was a bad parent, I was to blame. Never mind that Zach was an adult, he did not have the wherewithal to make such a decision. I should have prevented him from going paddling.

Unfortunately, I write to Zach, *I let this hurt me.* I should have dismissed it as a product of my family's turmoil. It shows me that in the aftermath of this tragedy people will be divided into three camps: those who feel it was a freak accident; those who blame the victims; and those who blame the parents. The blame game will surround Kaya and Zach's tragedy forever here on earth. *I will continue to protect you from unfair blame directed to you and Kaya even if it means that it is unfairly directed at us,* I write. *People have to find someone to blame when a tragedy occurs.*

* * *

We change our minds and decide to attend the convocation at which Zach would have received his Bachelor of Commerce, Honors Program. A friend who has helped us through some of the worst days since the tragedy, offers to drive us. Darlene represents Zach well although we are terribly sad that he is not there to accept the degree himself. During a different convocation later in the day, the dean notes Zach's passing, saying that he had the reputation of being a gentleman. To me, there is no higher compliment. It implies integrity, honesty, compassion, and responsibility, which were but a few of Zach's qualities. It would have been nice to hear this tribute at the earlier convocation when Zach's degree was presented, with us there to hear the dean's words.

Father's Day comes and goes, a day full of reflection. I start to compile my writings into a more organized format. I wonder whether I should expedite my writing. Will I be around long enough to do anything with it? I ask my spiritual guides for a sign. The reply, which I receive the next morning, is a bad mucus plug while lying in bed which requires immediate trach suction and twenty minutes of supplementary oxygen to help take away my shortness of breath. I ask the same question the next night and I am told the next morning that my friend Scott, a fellow ALS client, has passed in the night. I am not going to ask again. Nevertheless, I am organizing my writing in case something should occur more quickly than I anticipate. What happened to Zach and Kaya is all I require to appreciate that physical life is fragile even in the best of conditions.

Many of my writings are notes to Zach:

You and Kaya are constantly on our minds, as is finding happiness for Ben and Nathaniel. Your happiness, even in the spiritual world, we feel responsible for. We know that part of you feeling happiness is our ability to find happiness again. We acknowledge this and eventually will learn to do this, never forgetting you, but bringing our many happy memories with you to the forefront.

And:

I feel you around me, so I don't feel as lonely or sad as I could, but the tears are always close by should a thought trigger them. I have to avoid Hallmark movies for sure because they always make me cry.

I tell Zach how our first purchase for our second family home was a dining room set. He was only seven when we bought it. I wanted a table large enough to seat ten adults comfortably because in my mind I was setting places for myself, Darlene, each of the boys, their partners, and a pair of grandparents. I did not buy it for the now but for the future I envisioned. Too few years later, I was in a wheelchair and we did not use the table as no one was able to put the effort into a big family dinner requiring a dining room table. In recent years, because Zach was able to cook some great meals, we used the table again. Even though I could not cook or eat, I enjoyed the dinners and felt hopeful about future gatherings around the table. I am thankful to you for resurrecting our special family dinners around our dining room table, I write Zach, but from now on I will be reminded when sitting around it that two places will be forever empty.

CHAPTER FOURTEEN

At Six Months

THE LAST FEW WEEKS have been eventful. First, the good. We made a family visit to a new medium, a kind person who also lost an amazing child at a young age. This extremely talented medium began by bringing forward departed relatives with remarkable accuracy. This is the validation that is so important for us to know that Zach is communicating through her. He then spoke to Ben and Nathaniel, bringing forth messages about their present and immediate future. He told Darlene that he was with her in the "back room," the location of our master bedroom. He instructed me to keep talking to him and said that he will greet me in the afterlife along with my grandfather. He reaffirmed that he passed quickly because of the cold water, that he is with Kaya, that he is with us, that he loves us, and, most important, that he is happy. I feel that messages like this are all I require now.

The reading makes me question my purpose, especially with death lurking so close to me. I have been crying a lot and feeling hopeless again. I look back at an essay I wrote years ago about my hopes for my boys and their futures. I guess my hopes have not really changed significantly since then, despite all the change. Love endures even death. I question, as well, my identity. We have the choice of how we define ourselves, so what am I? A quadriplegic man who needs mechanical ventilation to survive? A bereaved parent clinging to sadness for two lives taken far too soon, robbing us of our present and our future? An active, caring, loving parent and husband? I suppose I am all three and probably more, but which identity is primary? If I define myself as the first and second, I will be overwhelmed by loss and never be happy and never honor the lives of Zach, Kaya, Ben, Nathaniel, and Darlene, to say nothing of my own. If I choose the third, I will have less suffering and will be able to live out my remaining time with a sense of purpose. It is important for us to choose positive self-definitions to steady us when we suffer reversals.

Now for the bad. I have a life-threatening complication after having an ERCP to help relieve a blockage in my biliary tract. I leave the hospital feeling a little discomfort from the outpatient procedure. At home the discomfort grows and then the vomiting starts. That night Darlene and the boys take me to our local hospital. The physician working that night does the necessary blood work and is shocked to see the profile of pancreatitis and possible infection of my biliary tract. He tells Darlene that he "is trying to get [me] through the night." Darlene is slapped in the face with my mortality.

I make it through the night and am transferred to our regional hospital and have an emergency procedure to put a stent across the blockage. Another week in the surgical ICU reinforces my opinion that the hospital is no place for a person with ALS who can't talk. I am so stoned on opioids that I can't even use my computer. Darlene, unable to leave my side, sees I'm not doing well in this setting and we decide to go home earlier than the doctor recommends.

I am home now, finally resting. On the radio, Dr. Maya Angelou is talking about her poem "Love Liberates," which has special meaning to Kaya and her mother. Both had the words "Love Liberates" inked onto their bodies months before the accident. At the time, those words kept them connected no matter where they were. Now the words connect all of us with Kaya and Zach. As Dr. Angelou is speaking, two light brown doves fly by my window. One hovers in front of me for a few seconds. I have never seen this bird before. I have never seen a bird other than my daily friends, the humming-birds, hover. In my old life, I would not have invested the appearance of these doves with significance. Today I know that Zach and Kaya are reaching out.

* * *

Most days I am able to write. One day I write well and leave off when I see a beautiful blue heron fly across my view over the river that Zach loved, as though he is showing himself to me. Other days I have to stop because I cannot see through the tears. Tears are the Kryptonite to my eye-tracking superpower. Still other days I draw a blank and even my nighttime talks with Zach become perfunctory. At these times, I merely give him updates. Nathaniel and Erica are in Bali. Nathaniel has grown a kick-ass beard. He will be going to Dalhousie University in the fall. Ben has decided to take the year off school and is working but not enjoying it. I worry for him. I think he will travel and try to find the right path for himself as he heals. I tell Zach we have been seeing Jennifer and Duncan regularly and I thank him and Kaya for putting us together.

The weather has been better and on bright days we sit on the deck. My eyes always go toward the purple bush where I saw Zach and Kaya holding each other for the last time as they gazed upon the river, its surface dancing with sunshine. The same spectacle remains there in front of me where the water is now one foot deep, giving the illusion of safety, peace, tranquility, much as it did back then. I see a clump of daisies that have bloomed in the last week and ask Darlene to put one in her hair, as I know Zach would have asked Kaya to do if they were here with us. Zach led us here, to this property. He loved the many beautiful perennials that are now in blossom, with more to come. Our renovations to the house and property are still not entirely finished. When they are, I will do my utmost to make the grounds a place where Zach and Kaya will want to visit, and where we will feel their presence in the peace and calmness of our natural setting. Right now, we are too heartbroken to feel it. Summer was the time of year Zach enjoyed most, a time for golf and friendship. It does not seem to matter how many days or weeks or months have passed. The loss of Zach and Kaya is persistent and pervasive. These feelings will never change. How else can you feel about the loss of your children? Regardless, I continue to note the numbers and the march of time. We pass twenty-one weeks. We lost them on February 21. They were both twenty-one years old.

We pass the two-year anniversary of my respiratory arrest. I think of the many variables that had to come to pass to put me in the hospital where they saved my life. A blocked feeding tube started my journey toward admission. The timing of my arrest was fortuitous, a weekday morning when everyone who was needed to help with a successful resuscitation was available. Even my own physician was immediately there to bring me back. Everything that could have ensured a successful recovery was in place for me to survive. *Why me?* That old question is flipped on its head. Why am I so lucky when nothing seemed to line up for Zach and Kaya?

* * *

Six months today and I am in despair. Everything came spiraling down to the ultimate truth. I have no hope for the future. It has been extinguished by ALS and Zach's departure. We cannot hope for a return to the activities we once enjoyed. Darlene has no reserves to make our lives a little richer or more diverse. Understandably, she has nothing more within herself to give freely without it costing her more than it is worth. I acknowledge this truth. I know that her health is paramount over my frivolous wants. And hope is extinguished.

This leads me to question, really and cruelly, for what purpose am I here? Darlene has been my caregiver for so long that we are not husband and wife anymore. I rarely help her because most of what I utter only wounds her. How many times have I heard her say to me, "That is the worst thing you could ever say to me"? Even if the conversation started with "How can I help you?" Are we doomed to mere existence with no hope for improvement? If that's the case and any betterment in my life can only come at great personal expense to Darlene, I have to ask again if my presence is selfish, if it is only hurting my family. I have believed until now that my family needed more stability before it was faced with further loss. Is that still the right answer?

* * *

We have had a crisis over the different ways we mourn. Darlene feels it is dishonorable to not talk about Zach and Kaya with every one of our friends. I choose to mourn with Darlene, the Firths, and the boys. I will honor Zach by mentioning pleasant memories when they come to me in conversation but I find it hard to talk about my grief. I appreciate Darlene's courage but for me it takes a lot of energy to be the bereaved father. Darlene is correct in this approach for her grief journey and this challenges me to reflect: I do feel I need to mourn more and not grieve in silence. She has also told me that I should not fall back on male/female stereotypes in my mourning because that has never been me in the past. We are far from experts in these matters, never having had great reason to mourn before. I do tend to fall for the ideal of "stay strong" in dealing with death, although when I'm with Darlene I can let my guard down and cry frequently.

I think Darlene is afraid that by not talking about Zach and Kaya openly with our friends, they will disappear from existence, and their lives will lose significance. My feeling is that they are part of us through shared memories and will therefore always be around their family and friends no matter how much or how little we display our mourning.

Both of our opinions reflect the genuine, individual responses of our fragile psyches to the agony of bereavement. Right now, hurtful things have been uttered each way. It is no wonder so many marriages break up after a loss of this magnitude. So much has changed since we said "I do" twenty-five years ago. Who could have foreseen a time when my movement around the house could only be accomplished through the expenditure of someone else's energy? Or that one of our sons would be ripped away from us in a senseless accident? This sadness will never be assuaged with time. It has changed who we are forever, and not in a good way. Now we are fragile shells of our former selves, trying to make it through the long, joyless days until we are medicated enough to get a few hours of restless sleep in separate beds before waking up and starting the same day over and over again.

We are in the depths of despair and nothing is going to get better for us until I am gone and Darlene can start again without the burdens of my ever-accumulating need. And even then, liberation will come at the price of more loss for Ben, Nathaniel, and most of all Darlene, for whom I would do anything in my limited power to protect from more pain.

All of this is intensified by Zach's birthday on August 26. One of his best buddies organizes a group of Zach's friends to write letters to us, sharing stories of the impact that Zach had on their lives. Another plants a plum tree outside of the man cave. These simple acts of caring for and acknowledgment of Zach are the only rays of light in our hopelessness.

I am trying to learn and grow through this process, with Darlene's help, although sometimes very reluctantly. I do want to close or at least bridge the sudden schism between us. Apart, we only feel more sadness, and more alone.

CHAPTER FIFTEEN

Thanksgiving

AUTUMN COMES, FIRST DABBING the tops of some of our trees with scarlet. We acknowledge more than celebrate our twenty-fifth wedding anniversary. Darlene has found a sculptor to make a statue of hummingbirds to replace my familiar friends who have packed up and left for warmer climes. We write each other letters and I make a soundtrack of our lives up to now. Ben and Nathaniel have left for Halifax in a brightly blue-and-pink-painted vintage Winnebago full of friends. "Winnie," as her owner affectionately calls his RV, has seen better days but I know it will get them to Halifax before Nathaniel's frosh week. After they get there, Ben is going to explore the East Coast. I am relieved that they feel secure enough about my health to enjoy their adventures without worrying about me.

As the leaves fall, I keep going back in my mind to my near-death experience, thinking of the silhouette of a boy's head. At the time, I named this image Josh. I now wonder if this last vision was of Zach. As a boy, I had an action figure named Big Josh whom Zach, with his close-cut beard at the time of my respiratory arrest, somewhat resembled. I do not know if this is a coincidence or of some spiritual significance. I expect I will find out when I leave my body.

I still talk with Zach but I've stopped obsessively chanting to myself the mantra that came to me when he passed: "They are free, they are love, they are together." Looking across the river, I see a few bare trees standing among the living: in nature, the dead coexisting with the living. Their purpose is to provide nourishment to sustain the living. I tell myself that Zach and Kaya are around us, nourishing our weakened souls. And then it is Thanksgiving. Both boys are in the house over the holiday weekend and while it is very hard to feel thankful for anything, we are grateful that we are together.

The house is finally finished although we still have some work to do to make it a home. Pictures need to be hung. Finishing touches here and there. We have designed it with many windows so you feel like you are amid nature in every room. With all its willows, birches, maples, walnut, spruces, and elms, the property is beautiful. Of course, the landscape is scarred by our loss but it is possible to see that in time this will be a home for Ben, Nathaniel, and us and, perhaps in time, for their families. In time the scar will not be as visible and new, happier memories might fill the house. Milestones will be celebrated, feasts attended, with thanks given for the wonderful things in our lives.

* * *

By the time we reach that eight-month mark, just after Thanksgiving, life is a little better. We still have days when our loss consumes us, days of endless tears, but they are less frequent than they were only a month ago. A little less of that extreme sadness pervades our home. Darlene can go into town now and feel safe there—small steps forward. Any positive movement is welcome in lives that grief has brought to a screeching halt.

We worry about Ben and Nathaniel as they continue with their healing. Ben is spending time in nature, exploring the many brooks around here for fish. Nathaniel, we think, likes university but gets overwhelmed at times and says he would prefer to be home. I do not know if he will continue after Christmas and I have come to the realization that he has to do it of his own volition. It is not for me to convince him. Darlene, Zach, and I wanted post-secondary educations. With Zach and Kaya gone, Ben and Nathaniel are questioning the need. They will do what they feel is best, recognizing that they can change direction at any time. The goal is happiness and love, not material success.

We continue to miss Zach and Kaya immensely. On most days we try to honor them and us by displaying the positive attributes of living full and meaningful lives. We know that longing for them will come and go during our lifetimes, whatever their durations. They will be a big part of our lives forever, and we know we can always find them by living in their realm of peace and love.

Many hours have been put into grieving the physical loss of them. We have explored and developed a set of beliefs that have helped us stay on the path of healing. We had to do this: otherwise, we would have stayed forever in the depths of despair. None of our beliefs are scientifically validated, nor will they be, but we carry them in our hearts and they bring us peace. Skeptics say that all mediums bring only messages of happiness and love. Perhaps, but these themes give us much comfort, and to us the messages appear validated through so many other facts known only by us. Grief has been a time of spiritual growth for us, a time of working to find the light again, non-judgmentally, through love and by integrating our losses into our "new" lives.

* * *

Dear Zach, I write as snow falls on the ground outside:

The winter solstice has just occurred, corresponding with the tenth month of you and Kaya not being physically in our lives.

In the months that followed your passing, I have tried using mantras and talking to you in my mind, in search of you. I have done some meditation, written and read to try to reach you and understand more of where you and Kaya might exist. I was fortunate to feel your presence leaning over me when I first came home from my hospital stay. It was during that event that I recognized you would always be there when I really needed you.

I have stayed open to the signs of nature around me and have seen your spirit in beavers, deer, doves, cardinals, blue jays and hummingbirds. . .

During our first conversation with you, through a medium, you told us you were okay, how much you loved us and how grateful you were for letting you live the life you wanted to live. You had one message for me, saying, "You can heal yourself from the inside." From this simple statement, I have explored books and myself to determine what set of beliefs I can integrate towards the "other side."

Now that Christmas approaches, I can state that Jesus was a great prophet who taught the positive attributes that we should strive to attain. He is the son of a divine presence that I will call God, but I know this entity incorporates the good in all religions. I also believe that all of us have a piece of this divine entity at our core so, really, we are all sons and daughters of this divine presence. I believe that love and peace should guide our lives. I believe that all is forgiven when we reach the "other side" and join the oneness of all life.

I know that without your teachings from the "other side" I would not have experienced this truth, but I would have preferred that my death would have taught these lessons to you and our family. I do recognize that the impact of my death would not have been the impetus to foster such change in others.

You and Kaya will be forever remembered for your goodness and abilities to bring happiness to all you have touched.

Love Dad

CHAPTER SIXTEEN

Anniversaries

SOMETHING UNEXPECTED HAPPENED IN the eleventh month of our mourning. The twenty-first of the month came and went without an acknowledgment by me, the first time this has happened since Zach's passing. Perhaps it was because Brent was here, or maybe the date is losing some of its terror for me. In any event, it is a relief to no longer be the victim of a date, or of time itself.

Much of our spiritual work has focused on resiliency. We know that wallowing in sorrow is not what our lost children want from us, and that it leads to life as a perpetual victim. We have been struggling to reach a higher plane and to inspire others who have suffered similar losses to find their resilience. With this in mind, we have decided to found an award in honor of Zach and Kaya to recognize young people who manage to keep going despite the horrendous darkness that has followed their loss of a loved one. Zach was resilient. As my health withered from ALS, he never asked for pity and rarely complained of how much it sucked being the person charged with doing more around the house than his friends. He just did it, and I think he enjoyed helping the family when he could. Kaya, although not faced with such a disease, did the same for her family and friends. It is our hope that helping others grieve in a manner that supports the growth of their souls will further the growth of our souls and put us on the path to appreciating happiness and joy again.

I write Zach again on the one-year anniversary of his passing, reminding him of how he showed me his scrambled eggs in a pot, and that I had seen him with Kaya, gazing out to the river, sharing an embrace and a kiss. I tell him how much his messages and spiritual presence have comforted us and promise that I will keep trying to speak with him, soul to soul. I might not be able to do this well until I shed my physical body but I will try:

> I grow weary of the fight some days, but I know I must spread your word of love. I will persevere for myself and our family until my time comes to join you and then we can work together to ease the pain of everyone we have been temporarily separated from.

I started taking notes in the fifth week of my grief, as a highly personal exercise, a form of therapy. It was an attempt at sorting and managing my emotions and thoughts in a desperate time. Although it has been mostly my individual journey, I now see broader lessons in it. It is possible for people to survive and eventually find a measure of peace with grief, even under the extreme circumstance of a coexisting terminal disease. Life is never extinguished by our physical deaths. It just changes.

CHAPTER SEVENTEEN

A Prescription for Grieving

WHEN I WAS GROWING UP, people did not want to discuss cancer. Stiff upper lip and all that. Now, in general, people will talk about cancer and support a person's individual fight against cancer with walks, galas, and social media campaigns. Grief feels to me as though it is back where cancer used to be, a taboo subject. People have no vocabulary for it, no structured way to express what they are experiencing or to talk about the loss with the affected person. They hide their feelings and try to ignore the event, afraid that discussion of the physical death of a loved one will elicit an emotional breakdown in the people most affected by the loss. In my experience, this approach is antiquated and fails to help the bereaved. I have learned through experience that we want to hear the names of our lost loved ones and that we honor them and keep them alive in our hearts and minds through talking about them.

It is time to write a new prescription for how to healthily grieve so that we are clear on what helps and what may unintentionally hurt when we grieve or try to support those grieving.

1. Avoid certain words and phrases. Telling an individual who has lost a loved one that he or she is strong is meant as a compliment. However, to some in the early stages of grief it can be taken in another manner. It is no comfort to hear how strong we are or that you would be unable to be as strong in our shoes. We are torn apart inside in ways you cannot see. We need to do a lot of our grief work alone and with those who directly share our loss. Strength, and the inability to have strength if the roles were reversed, can imply that we did not love our loved one as much as you would have loved your loved ones, otherwise we would appear more distraught. We maintain our composure to support our families. To crumble would cause more tragedy now or in the future.

   What we refer to as strength in later phases of grief is a misnomer. A better word to describe the ability of someone to reconcile and integrate the loss of a loved one and forge ahead with peace and purpose in his or her life is resilience. Being seen as resilient is a compliment to the bereaved because it implicitly acknowledges the hard work that a person has done on the grief journey.

   The phrase *Thoughts and prayers* has become so commonplace that it has lost meaning and is reflexively put on bereavement cards and offers little comfort. Spend a few thoughtful moments composing your messages of condolence. Sometimes people use comparatives such as *I know how you feel because I have lost my own. . .* It is well intended but everyone has different relationships with their loved one. You cannot compare losses based solely on the name of the family relations.

   The phrase *He/she is better off now* should also be avoided. The ones who have passed do not need comfort. It is the ones left behind who need our compassion. Yes, of course, in some cases the terminally ill suffer immensely before they succumb and pass. By saying they are better off, you assume that the bereaved shares your view of the afterlife, which is not always the case.

With the numerous phrases that one uses to console the grieving (I have just mentioned a few), the important theme is to never minimize their loss. Ultimately, the bereaved require you to hold space for them.

2. Avoid *Hi, how are you?* Most people really do not want to know how we are doing. The truth is we are destroyed. Whatever happened to simply saying hello? No one ever answers *How are you?* truthfully, in any event. To the bereaved, the question is troubling: it makes them think that they must express how terrible they feel in order to do justice to their lost beloved, yet they do not have the energy or the desire to talk about it. *Hi* is sufficient, perhaps adding the phrase, *I am truly sorry for your loss.* When you really want to know how we are, sit with us in an intimate setting and ask. We do not expect you to have an answer. We just need you to listen.

3. Acknowledge the departed. We decided early in our grief that we would include the names of all three sons in letters we wrote as a family. Zach is spiritually present in our lives, so signing his name and writing *(in spirit)* after it acknowledges both his physical reality and his ongoing participation in our family. Our hope is that people will follow our lead.

   During our first Christmas without Zach, family and friends sent seasonal cards wishing us the best over the holidays. Only one that we received mentioned our dear son, probably because people on the sending end did not know how to acknowledge Zach. Of course, we would not have known any better how to do it before our loss. If I could have advised the people writing those cards, I would have said please acknowledge Zach as a member of the family. It is a simple gesture, but a meaningful one to us. As our grief and beliefs have evolved, so, too, has our method of acknowledgment. We have dropped *(in spirit)*. The important thing is to follow the lead that a family has established to acknowledge their departed loved one.

4. Never blame, shame, or judge. Why do we tend to blame something or someone for physical deaths? Of course, there are instances of murder and manslaughter where blame is warranted but in most deaths, there should be no blaming of those who die or of family members who survive.

In our case, Zach and Kaya were blamed. Some people believe they were irresponsible for kayaking in the middle of February and not wearing life jackets. They know nothing of the river or the conditions that day or the capabilities and good judgment of the victims. Looking at anything retrospectively gives us information that might have helped divert tragedy but life occurs in the now, with people making the best decisions they can with the information they have.

I have been blamed for the accident because I should have known better than to allow a twenty-one-year-old to take such a risk. The person who blamed me for allowing Zach to kayak in winter went on to cite evidence that the brain does not fully mature until a human is twenty-five, suggesting that I should have overruled Zach's judgment with my own. Yet we allow these supposedly underdeveloped brains to drive cars, fight wars, vote, and decide their own futures. Zach, Ben, and Nathaniel were raised in an environment that if anything encouraged early maturity. As Ben, who was then nineteen, said just after the accident, "There will always be accidents because we are unable to predict every circumstance that puts us at risk."

People pass judgment to protect and distance themselves from fatal accidents as if by drawing simple conclusions they can ward off tragedy from their own family. This is delusional.

Judging is a human weakness (and I recognize the irony of judging judgment as a weakness).

Shame can accompany a tragedy defined by mental health problems, especially suicide. Surviving family members have to deal with it. Depression is an illness and, as a result, victims who end their lives through suicide, usually, but not always, after severe and prolonged suffering, see no choice in the matter. People who suffer from mental health illness are experts at hiding the true extent of their suffering. They often appear better just before succumbing to their mental health illness because they finally see the end of their suffering and are at peace. There should be no shame visited upon victims of suicide or their loved ones. I am not saying that severe cases of depression are hopeless. I have seen dramatic results for those people who persevere with illness and eventually find the "right" treatment and support.

Mental illness did not play a role with Zach and Kaya, but I have experienced severe and prolonged suffering, and I know how someone could contemplate suicide. My trials, fortunately, have not been on par with those of people who ultimately succumb. There could be a time in the future, however, when I might see medical assistance in dying as the only escape from the immensity of my suffering. If this should occur, I would hope that no one in my family, including myself, is shamed because of my decision.

Those are just a few suggestions for how to talk to grieving people. Here is one for the grieving themselves: no regrets. *I should have returned his call. I should have told her I was sorry. I should have said "I love you" more often.* This litany of should-haves can go on and on. We did not really have any 'should haves' in our relationship with Zach. Due to my illness and even before that, *love you* was a common phrase in our home. The boys and I would write personal birthday letters to each other and Darlene would spend hours trying to find the perfect card. The boys knew how much we loved them. Because we were so consciously preparing for a time in the future when I would not be present in their lives, I can honestly say there are no regrets in our relationships with any of the boys.

At the same time, I have agonized over every decision in my life that might have contributed to Zach and Kaya's tragedy. I know that these should-haves and what-ifs will never be quelled so I choose not to dwell among them for long. When I do find that I have allowed myself to go there, I know that I will never find peace. Our brains are equipped to produce negative thought patterns that can quickly invent self-blame where none reasonably exists. When I go to these depths, I can only escape my thoughts by taking a pause. I step out of my brain and become an observer of the traps my thoughts are creating. By acting as an observer, I can eventually acknowledge that my thoughts tend to emphasize my fears and doubts and are not the real me. When we recognize the disconnect between our thoughts and our true selves, we begin healing and we banish the blame that our should-haves forces upon us.

Living with expressions of love will eliminate some of our regrets but ultimately it is only by recognizing the harm we do with our thought patterns and our false blaming of ourselves that we will release ourselves from the infinity of should-haves and what-ifs that fester in our thoughts after the death of our beloved.

* * *

Every bereaved person has had family or friends who manage to say the one thing or behave in the one way that seems unfathomable to you. We are likely to forgive the words or the action eventually, but we will never forget how it made us feel in the moment.

The psychologist Susan Silk has developed what she calls the Ring Theory to help friends and family successfully navigate times of loss.

Silk places the person most directly impacted by the loss at the core. This person (or people) should receive comfort only from those further from the loss. This core person is permitted to unload on anyone outside the core without judgment or consequence. The theory also states that the "core" should receive love and support from anyone outside the "core." Surrounding the core person (or people) is the ring of people next affected by the loss. People in this ring can give comfort to those in the core, and receive comfort from those outside their ring, and they are able to unload on people outside their ring without judgment or consequence. These rings go outward and outward, always obeying the rule of comforting inward and unloading outward.

Most of us understand this innately but some of us do not, or forget it in the moment, or feel ourselves exceptions to it, and problems arise as a result. My greatest disappointment in dealing with the two great losses I have suffered occurred when these simple rules were not followed by family or those who used to be close friends. When I was diagnosed with ALS, we unloaded on people in our outer rings expecting support and comfort; instead, some people dumped on us. This led to estrangements. Failure to abide by the rules can destroy friendships and wreck families. If it happened to my family, as it did with my older brother, my parents, and a judgmental relative, it can happen to any family. Fortunately, most of these relationships have been partially repaired by saying *I am sorry* and gestures of generosity and compassion.

From my personal experience, I would add to Silk's schematic three more phenomena. First, each person who suffers a loss will be the core in their loss, requiring the support of their friends more distant from the loss. Second, it is important not to overlook the sometimes forgotten mourner, the friend of a deceased person who

did not have a familial connection but perhaps was closer to him
or her than family members. Finally, rings can thin and disappear,
especially when people are living with chronic disease. The outer
rings may fade away as people decide to leave your life. Sometimes
people in the inner rings make the same decisions, usually because of
their own issues more than yours. Excessive unloading can contribute to this phenomenon. Those in my closest rings try not to dump
outward too often, as do I.

* * *

How often do we hear about the five stages of grief, otherwise known
as the Kübler-Ross model? It postulates that a terminally ill patient
will, after diagnosis, experience, in this order: denial, anger, bar-
gaining, depression, and acceptance. The model is controversial
even in the specific instances of people diagnosed with terminal illnesses. It does not apply to people in grief over the death of a loved
one. There are no defined stages in grief. Many people, ourselves
included, experience nonlinear grief, with many emotions present-
ing in random sequence or coexisting. Some of the worst emotions
can eventually coexist with happiness and joy. Grief is highly personal and is influenced by support, environment, cause of death, age
of death, out-of-order death, and the personal relationship you had
with the loved one who passed on, among other factors. Generally,
if a person is given time, support, and space, he or she will be able
to do the individual work necessary to accept loss. Time to grieve
a tragic loss is important for people but still most are only given a
few days off work; this will have to be reassessed in the future. As
Kaya's mom, Jennifer, has said, "[In Canada] Mothers and fathers are
given up to eighteen months' leave from work when a child enters
a family, why do they only get a few days off when a child leaves a
family? "

We have found a useful metaphor for grief in the conch shell. At the sharp end of the conch, there are tight spirals of shell development, just as in the early stages of grief there are intense emotional episodes one after the other, almost to the point that it feels constant. We are spinning in grief, barely in control of ourselves. With time, support and emotional work, we continue to experience grief but not so intensely and often, so the spirals become elongated, as seen in the lengthening of the spirals of a conch shell. While the grief keeps coming and can be overwhelming at times, its duration continues to shorten and the episodes become less frequent and can eventually even coexist with moments of happiness and normality.

Another misconception about grief is that "time heals all." We have found that time only helps if you put work into the personal growth necessary to live beyond your loss. For us that has meant opening ourselves to influences we would not have consulted in the past. We have read voraciously, scoured the Internet, listened to inspirational talks and messages, consulted mediums, and followed our own instincts to slowly evolve our own set of beliefs that feel right for us. We have taken what we have found good and useful from all major religions without dogma and politics. The grieving need to find their own belief systems. For some, that may mean relying on their existing religious beliefs. For others, like us, it may require a deep process of reconciling new spiritual beliefs with your own sense of truth. I will address our spiritual journey more comprehensively in another chapter.

The last misconception about grief that I will mention is the notion that it is a journey with a destination. While each of our paths through grief is different, there are similarities and the largest is that the journey will not end in your lifetime. Nevertheless, with work and time, you will be able to integrate the grief into the rest of your life and if you are successful at this, the depths of your sadness will not be as deep as before and the periods of sadness will not last as long—they will be mixed or interspersed with lighter emotions—but you will still carry your grief. This is the most for which we can hope.

* * *

I have come to the realization that support groups, designed to allow you to speak with others who are on similar journeys, are well-intentioned and helpful to people experiencing any type of loss. Personally, I never involved myself with a regular ALS support group by choice. It seemed unlikely that I would benefit from being grouped with strangers with whom I had nothing in common but a disease. I knew that ALS affects families very differently depending on age. Could I have empathy for a person who was dealing with the illness at seventy when I was diagnosed at forty-one? Could a younger man of, say, twenty-seven empathize with me when I had at least been healthy enough to start a career and a family and see them grow? I was fortunate to have great support from friends and I was receiving one-on-one support from a person with ALS. Personally, one-on-one is my preferred support model and I have tried to offer it to others with ALS but, again, everyone must choose the path that supports their needs.

Awful as it sounds to say this, there was one fortunate side effect to Zach and Kaya passing together. My family and Kaya's family shared very similar experiences. Zach and Kaya were both completely and unconditionally loved during their physical lives, and neither family had regrets with them. Although we had no social relationship before the accident, and it would not have been unusual for the two families to isolate themselves in its wake, Darlene and I immediately formed a support group with Jennifer and Duncan. At our first meeting a few days after the event, we all felt the benefit of grieving for our children together, and we have been fortunate to grow through our individual grief at similar rates. Each of us put in a tremendous amount of work toward healing, initially five to eight hours together every week, and another twenty hours apart. The effect on our healing has been tremendous.

Support groups bring people together who have experienced similar struggles. The group supports its members by saying, *Yes, we understand how you are feeling, we have felt the same in our experiences.* Groups also allow for peer mentorship. Persons with more experience of the circumstance can help others who are newer to it with practical advice that has proven useful to them. In the case of losing a child, they are also useful because the loss can stigmatize and isolate parents. We have seen this firsthand with friends who no longer call because they cannot handle the tragedy we face daily.

In order for support groups to do their best for participants, I believe certain criteria need to be met. This includes an experienced and responsive facilitator and a useful frequency of meetings. I question the healing that can occur in groups that meet monthly without great individual work. There need to be continuous opportunities within the meetings for individuals and the group to grow. I worry when support groups become more like a club that you never want to join but attend simply for a lack of alternatives. Finally, there should be a time when the individual member "graduates" from the group, and perhaps starts to meet with smaller groups of people, outside the bereavement support group, people with whom they feel a connection. Caroline Myss, an author who writes about what she terms "woundology," warns that people can get stuck in loss. Woundology can simply be defined as when a person holds on to their adversity because by doing so they experience secondary gains. For example: Who would want to heal if by doing so you would no longer be supported by the group? Hence the need to graduate at some point back into the world of the living. You will never ever completely heal from significant loss, but you do have the choice of whether or not you will forever be a victim of your loss.

* * *

A final point about grieving. I have read many books along the way, some of which gave me peace, some of which made me ask myself dark questions, and some of which made me look at people differently. Dr. Susan A. Berger's *The Five Ways We Grieve* allowed me to recognize the general patterns in which people grieve, and how these affect the future life of the bereaved. We may at first fall into a number of categories that Dr. Berger defines but eventually we will find one that gives us the support we need.

To briefly summarize Dr. Berger's work. The Nomads are people with unresolved grief and no anchor of security or stability. The Memorialists find peace with grief by honoring the memory of their lost loved ones with concrete objects, rituals, or tributes that recognize the departed by name. Normalizers feel that the most important result of their loss is to make things better for themselves and their families, now and in the future. They ultimately desire normality and to recapture parts of their lives as they were before their loss. Activists are brought by bereavement to an acute understanding of the finite nature of existence and want to do something positive, such as making the world a better place, for the remainder of their lives. For Seekers, loss prompts philosophical inquiry about the meaning and purpose of life and brings the bereaved to value connections with other people, the natural world, and the divine.

During my loss with ALS, my mantra was to live as normally as possible for the well-being of myself and my family, in the present and, for my family, in their future without me. I was also an activist for ALS, raising money for support services and research with the goal of ridding the world of the disease. I would place myself evenly in both categories as they pertain to ALS.

For my greater loss, that of Zach and Kaya, I can see myself in each category. I was first a Nomad, drifting and mostly stuck in my grief. During my low days, I still return to this purgatory, although less frequently than before. We are Memorialists through our establishment of the Zach Sutherland and Kaya Firth Resiliency Scholarship. Spending countless hours blinking out words to help and inspire others dealing with loss is my Activist behavior (and, I suppose, another act of memorialization for Zach and Kaya, and perhaps even for myself). The Normalist in me wants my family to recover and works purposefully to make life better for them today and tomorrow. Finally, the Seeker in me has developed a new relationship with the Divine.

I have grieved in many distinct ways and have not settled yet into a distinct category but I do trust Dr. Berger's assertion that in time we all relate primarily to one group. While each has its pros and cons, the one that concerns me most is the Nomads, the lost people who become stuck in grief. I believe that this category of griever—and most of us pass through the Nomad group in the early stages of our loss—will benefit most from Dr. Berger's book and from mine.

CHAPTER EIGHTEEN

Old Beliefs

I T IS OFTEN THROUGH adversity that we are challenged to grow spiritually. Darlene and I grew through ALS, adapting to our new circumstances early and readily, with love and positive mindsets, yet our further loss made us grow far more—in fact, more than I thought was possible in one lifetime. There is nothing like tragic loss to challenge your beliefs.

I was brought up in the United Church of Canada. My mother was Anglican and my father was United and an elder in the church. I remember going with him on Saturday afternoons to cut cubes of white bread and prepare grape juice from concentrate, the essentials of the next day's communion. The bread would be put on silver trays and the grape juice would fill about three hundred shot glasses. I was proud of my father's participation. I attended Sunday School where we read stories from the Bible. Through these stories, I was introduced to a confusing God. How could God be both vengeful and merciful? Because the preaching of Jesus became our primary teaching, I learned about forgiveness and love. *Love* was the answer I would give to any question posed by my Sunday School teacher. I knew that by answering with this word I would always be at least partially correct.

My family was active in the church in our early years but, like most other families I knew, our participation lagged as my brothers and I grew and other activities seemed more important. By my early teens, I was going to confirmation classes before church with two good friends and afterward skipping Sunday service to walk to a doughnut shop and then home. I enjoyed this time with my friends. Not long after my confirmation in grade nine, I became one of those Christmas and Easter parishioners. High school sports and, later, university and medical school dominated my schedule. I did not abandon religious feeling. I was drawn to epic biblical movies from the 1950s and the music from Andrew Lloyd Webber's *Jesus Christ Superstar*. I believed God was a part of me and I understood that my sense of right and wrong had been molded by Christian morality.

Darlene and I were married in my family church by the female minister who had recently come to lead the congregation. We chose my church because Darlene, after moving to a newer community from where she grew up, did not have a spiritual home. She was raised Roman Catholic. We felt that the Catholic church was too exclusive in who it allowed to participate in the sacrament of communion, and we objected to its position on women in the ministry and numerous other of its rites and beliefs. We knew we could not promise to raise our children in this faith.

After we were married, I was too busy with my residency to consider going to church (although another resident managed to keep up his observance). Three years later, Zach entered our lives and we began looking for a church to call home. Our first attempt was a local United Church. During our first service there, the lay minister announced that the minister had been arrested for indecent exposure and would not be returning. We tried another church the following Sunday.

This second effort was at an established Anglican church. The Anglican faith was not foreign to either of us. We each had a grandmother who had been involved in her local Anglican parish throughout her life. At the eleven o'clock service, we were surrounded by about twenty people, all twice our age. Zach started crying around fifteen minutes into the mass, understandable for an eight-month-old. After five minutes of failing to console him, we decided to slip out as inconspicuously as three people can from a small gathering. As we were exiting the building, the priest put the service on hold and left the sanctuary to have a quick word with us. This kind man welcomed us to his church and suggested that the nine thirty a.m. service, which included a nursery, was more suitable for young families. Grateful for the priest's courtesy, we made his church our new spiritual home. We attended whenever my emergency-room schedule permitted.

We developed an extended church family at this parish, meeting families who became good friends. I was asked to be a chalice bearer. About a month after Ben was born, we had both Zach and Ben baptized. Nathaniel came along fourteen months later and he, too, was eventually baptized, although in a different manner. Toward the end of our priest's time at the parish, he wanted to end his performance of the baptismal rite in the manner in which he had started his ministry so long ago in Jamaica, where parishioners were baptized in a river. And so, during the priest's last service with us, in the midst of the church picnic, Nathaniel was baptized and welcomed to the teachings of Christianity in the shallow Credit River. The same river in which we would lose Zach and Kaya fifteen years later.

I enjoyed communion in the Anglican Church. I found singing the responses to the sacrament of communion a truly spiritual experience. It was my type of meditation. The boys' competitive hockey took us away from church as a family for five years—like many others their age, my sons did not think they needed the church at that time in their lives—but I continued attending alone as a chalice bearer and lay reader. After my diagnosis of ALS, I continued my duties at the parish for as long as I could. My last service as a chalice bearer was during the Christmas Eve service in 2008. I had to use the little handrail to climb the three small steps to the altar. Thankfully, even in my weakened state, I never dropped the "blood of Christ."

In early January of 2015, I was asked by Rob, our reverend, to give the sermon at our church. By this time, I had been in a wheelchair for six years, and I had been on my permanent ventilator for five months. With Darlene, Zach, Ben, and Nathaniel by my side, I spoke to the congregation:

> When Rob asked me if I wanted to write something for church, I think I surprised him with how quickly I wanted to wrestle the pulpit from him. . . . I thought about what I could say to you that you have not already heard before from far wiser people than me.
>
> I remembered being told that the secret to preventing people from falling asleep when you are speaking is to tell stories. I have three little stories that happened to me in the last few years that I would like to share with you.

The first story involved Reverend Canon Rob Park and our twenty-one-year-old cat. We had gotten Amore and her sister, Ariel, after our honeymoon. Ariel had died at age fifteen but Amore was still kicking around. Rob and Wendy had visited us for Easter communion in 2012. Poor old Amore was not doing well. She was probably on her tenth life. She had lost weight. A friend called her "zombie cat." We comforted her and kept her close but we knew she was fighting to keep going. When Rob asked us if there was anyone he could say a prayer for, we suggested Amore, knowing that our life-long companion needed help to let go. Rob humored us, although I think he thought we were crazy. He gave a blessing and prayer for Amore. Not five minutes after Rob had left for his next home visit,

I watched Amore take a deep breath. It was her last breath. What a fortunate event for all concerned, to have her pass away naturally amid her family.

My second story was about an infamous Christmas ice storm in 2013. The Saturday evening before Christmas, we were getting into our van for a friend's Christmas party. As we left, we noticed our Christmas lights go off. The whole neighborhood was dark. We continued on our way to our friend's place, thinking that the power would be quickly restored. Instead the freezing rain continued and so much ice accumulated on the trees that by ten o'clock you could hear the eerie sound of heavy branches snapping from trunks. By eleven, we knew we would have to face our house without power. "You probably wouldn't know it by looking at me," I joked to the congregation, "but I am very dependent on electricity."

> I need it to charge my computer that allows me to talk, power my chair so I can move, and at that time, before my ventilator, I needed it to power my BiPap machine, so I could breathe easily when sleeping. In our home, I need electricity to power my elevator to take me upstairs to our bedroom. Without power, I would have to be carried upstairs by my friends who had probably had a little too much Christmas cheer.

Obviously, this caused me anxiety. I envisioned them dropping me halfway up the staircase. We were just about to make the transfer from my wheelchair into the hands of my inebriated friends when the electricity came on. Darlene and Zach sprang into action and got me in the elevator and upstairs. After I was safely aloft, the power went off again just as suddenly as it had come on. Expecting that we were in for a long outage, a friend on Sunday morning scoured nearby Brampton to buy us one of the last available gas generators. With that and multiple extension cords, we were quite comfortable upstairs in our bedroom. I don't think I have ever entertained so many people in our bedroom. Four days and nights passed until the power returned just before Christmas Day and I could go downstairs again. During that spell, the power had only been available for five minutes. I was very fortunate that that sliver of power came exactly when I needed it, and also to have a friend with the foresight to find a generator for my family.

My third story was of my respiratory arrest the previous August, which had occurred in a hospital at a time when all the critical responders were present and ready to face a crisis. I shared the three stories, each with a similar theme, for a reason:

Some might characterize the theme as a person having good fortune. The best, of all the endless possibilities, occurred on each of these occasions. What if it wasn't purely luck? Could there be another explanation for these fortunate events? Could there have been some divine presence looking over me and my family? Good fortune or small miracles—that is the question that remains to be answered by each of us.

I think we can all think of similar situations when everything has lined up for us and we have experienced extremely good fortune without questioning how it occurred. Maybe all of those lucky events were moments when God was helping us find a safe passage, events when God was actively participating in our lives, even if we weren't able to fully appreciate it.

Good fortune or small miracles? I think it depends on if you are able to believe in the power of God. We have to believe in miracles to see them occur in our lives.

The prayer after communion comes to my mind. During that, we all recite, "Glory to God, whose power working in us can do infinitely more than we can ask or imagine." Do we truly believe in what we are saying?

I prefer to believe that God is watching out for each of us. That belief gives me strength and comfort.

Please join me for a little prayer: Thank you, God, for looking over us and our families. For giving us the resources to want to be alive, loving and supportive families, a welcoming church community, and great friendships. Finally, thank you for enabling us to see the many miracles that occur in our lives. Amen.

Otherwise unable to attend services, I continued to take communion from Rob on his visits during Easter and Christmas. After my respiratory arrest and near-death experience, however, my traditional religious views began to fade. Many people are familiar with Christopher Hitchens's opinions on the afterlife. He is the ultimate skeptic on the existence of consciousness after physical death. His opinions, like mine, have no scientific validity, nor will they ever be anything more than personal opinions, yet for a time after my arrest—after I had failed to see the expected light—I was beginning to share them.

Losing Zach and Kaya took me further from my traditional beliefs and made me question an "all-seeing" and benign deity, one that rewards good moral behavior with a happy ending. I talked in my sermon about the many small miracles that had happened in my life. Why were Zach and Kaya not granted the same grace from God when they needed it? In the earliest days after our greatest loss, I wrote to my God:

Why did you take our son and Kaya?

Why did you give me the intellect, drive, empathy, and skills to be a good physician and then take my calling away?

Why did you give us three beautifully unique boys, each growing up with a close bond that goes beyond siblings, and take one away?

Why did you take along with our son his "most important person in his world?"

Why did you make our children lose their innocence at the tender ages of 13, 11, and 10 as ALS came into our lives?

Why did you allow them to be empathetic, supportive and loving to us and each other just to have their oldest brother perish during an activity with such a mundane risk?

Why did I have to lose extended family with each personal loss?

Why did you not give my oldest brother the emotional intelligence to take an active role in our lives when ALS attacked our family?

Why did you not give my parents the skills to help my nuclear family grieve when they were most needed?

Why, when life was just again starting to have hope for me, did you extinguish it for us all?

Why does our family have to again be the center of a tragedy and this time have to carry the tragedy for the rest our lives?

Why does a family which is inherently good have to deal with so much bad?

Why does my wife who has shown to have reserves beyond compare have to deal with the loss of her firstborn who had grown into an incredible young man?

Why did you save me a year ago just to lead us to the river where this tragedy occurred?

Why us? Why us? Why us!

CHAPTER NINETEEN

New Beliefs

A FTER MY LETTER TO GOD, I knew that Christianity alone could not help me make sense of our losses. Its conception of the Divine—the angry, punishing God of the Old Testament, the loving and forgiving God of the New Testament—has served a purpose for millennia, bringing discipline, comfort, and hope to believers. But in my lifetime there has been a great shift in religiosity in the Western World as new generations struggle with the dogmas of the past, with the father-son relationship that is at the core of the great religions, with their tendency to divide people through their laws and other constrictions. As we have become more enlightened, we have reached for a new construct of God and the Divine. I know that this will not be well received by everyone but to me, it is almost common sense.

After the physical passing of Zach and Kaya, I found that I wanted to use every religion to form my spiritual beliefs. I would not be tied to a specific religion's teachings. I would create my own truths by taking what seemed to me universal in every religion: love, peace, and oneness with our Creator and all life. Through seemingly random occurrences (which I now believe are spiritual manifestations) and the use of people gifted in communication with departed souls, I came to believe that consciousness does exist after physical life ends, that Zach and Kaya still exist in a spiritual form, that they know how we are doing and what we are doing, and that the energy of their souls resides on a plane close to us. This belief has given me comfort and the ability not to fear my eventual death. And should that not be the ultimate goal of any belief system: to not hurt others, and to give us hope?

To reflect this new reality, I wrote out my new beliefs twelve weeks after our tragedy:

I believe that there are contracts before souls come to earth. These are made between many souls that are together for the benefit of the group. They are in place to define what experiences the soul must experience before it can progress to higher levels in heaven.

I believe in a layered heaven and that we all go where our souls fit best.

I believe in soul karma and that it follows souls through several lifetimes.

I believe that there are non-physical helpers and teachers that we have to talk to, and ask for guidance.

I believe in a Creator. This is a pure energy from which all souls are created.

I believe that the Creator is not responsible for our physical lives and the tragedies and catastrophes that occur in them.

I believe we get what we give. If we give the positive energies of love, compassion, trust, and forgiveness, we will receive this back. If we give the negative energies of anger, fear, and sorrow, we will receive this back.

I believe that we all have spiritual partners.

I believe that when we die, we graduate, and go back home.

I believe that our passed loved ones are able to talk to us through dreams and how we feel. Mediums can be used for more direct communication.

I believe that every soul has exit points and the soul unbeknownst to the body prepares for their departures.

I believe that I can heal myself from within in a spiritual way.

I believe in multiple universes and multiple life forms throughout these universes.

I believe that love is the sole principle of life both in the physical and spiritual dimensions.

I believe that Zach and Kaya were old souls and that is why they were here for a short time.

I believe that they were higher spirits who did not have much to learn during this physical lifetime.

I believe that they are spiritual partners and have been together for multiple lifetimes.

I believe that when we pass from this lifetime that we will unite with their souls again.

I know that life will go on without their physical presence and that they will be forever in my thoughts.

Now, three years after I recorded those beliefs, I continue to hold them. Now I name '*heaven*' as *the other side*, which to me seems more inclusive.

Significant loss is accompanied by significant change. If you do not change with your loss, you will get stuck in your grief. I still believe in the Divine, but I no longer see the Divine as a single entity. Rather, I see it as something more complex, if not infinite. The Christian notion of the Divine as a single being first emerged in the Book of Genesis, written at a time when humanity had yet to develop the ability to probe the intricacies of the body and mind. God was one entity and, according to Genesis, people were made in God's image, as single entities, too. We now know that the human body is not one thing. It is made of trillions of separate entities called cells, and we also know that cells are made of countless elements and that these elements are made of countless subatomic particles. We are a network of innumerable particles working in unison for the good of our physical bodies. This seems to me an appropriate analogy for a new understanding of the Divine. It is consistent with Genesis in that we are still made in the image of the Divine but it accounts for a better understanding of our reality.

From this, I envision the Divine as a network of countless collective spirits who have ascended to an ultimate good. They represent the internal goodness in all conscious life. I do not believe that this God has an ability to affect life on earth or in any other nonspiritual domain. I do believe that this complex entity prepares individual spirits for the circumstances and trials that they must face in their physical forms. In our physical forms, we freely choose how to respond when confronted with life's challenges and opportunities, and it is on these individual paths that our souls grow or do not grow.

Also central to my beliefs is the existence of an "other side" comprised of infinite space. In this space are only love and a feeling of connection with all consciousness and all life through every universe. The human concepts of time, gender, and form do not exist. We are all connected to this other side by the spark of divinity each living thing possesses. That divinity is pure energy. This can bear whatever name you prefer: God, Allah, Jesus, Buddha or any non-secular name. The message is that the divinity does not grant one group special rights over others. Divinity is one with all, inclusive to its core.

The other side exists, right here and right now, on a different dimension where conscious spirits reside when not in physical form. Most of us cannot experience this dimension. We are too caught up in our material worlds and have little motivation to explore our spirituality sufficiently to reach the other side. My reading suggests that most people do not arrive at new beliefs passively. Rather, they are aggressively pushed to reconsider their faiths by significant personal loss. Some will find solace in traditional religious beliefs while others, unable to find answers in a single religion, will incorporate messages from different faiths into their own belief systems, as I have done. Most will adopt some version of what might be the core message of religion: love your neighbor as yourself. This principle seems to bring us closest to divinity. I would argue, in fact, that it *is* divinity, the higher life to which all of us should aspire.

Zach and Kaya have given us many messages from the other side through the help of various spiritual mediums. These messages are always brought after the mediums have validated who they are communicating with. Validation is the key to building trust with your spiritual guide. The medium names distant relatives, describes the layout of our home, describes Zach and Kaya and their core values and describes recent events only we could know about. We all have scientific minds and tend to be critical thinkers so we require a good deal of validation before we accept that we are connecting with the nonphysical entities of our children. Not every reading has rung true. Some spiritual mediums are better than others. Like all groups of people, some are exceptional, others are amateurs or even worse, people who do not have your best interests at heart and most lie on the spectrum in between. On a cautionary note, if you are grieving, and therefore very vulnerable, we suggest that you get a referral from a person you trust before consulting with a spiritual medium.

Most people would not seek spiritual mediums except when dealing with incredible grief. As a physician, I have always believed comfort can come from many different sources, so long as no harm is done to yourself or others. It is not up to me to decide what is true for people in very different circumstances from my own. In our case, we have found comfort in the messages brought to us. Zach describes the other side "as beautiful" and says that he and Kaya are connected to all life there. They are together. Love surrounds them. As a parent, all that I wish for my children is that they are happy, and Zach in his spiritual state is happy, as he was in his physical state. He and Kaya are around us and their friends practically all the time.

Zach wants to be remembered for the happy life he lived, not for the circumstances of his death. He says that his death was predetermined and only through the choices that he had at the time could he exert his free will. He wants us to heal from their physical loss and he wants us to know that he will always be part of our physical lives until that point of time in which our physical lives revert back to the spiritual and at that time he will be there to welcome us to the purely spiritual. On the other side, Zach is a healer. He uses his critical thinking to improve processes and helps souls just entering the other side adapt to their new circumstances. He has taken after me in this regard, but his place of practice is in the spiritual realm.

The overall themes of happiness, predetermination, oneness with all, and, most important, love, are messages that all of us need to hear when grieving the physical loss of loved ones. Having faith that we will all be together again means that the loss is temporary. Having faith that our loved ones are still here but in a different dimension can lessen our sense of loss.

I know some readers will feel that I have lost my evidence-based mind but my beliefs and the messages they provide seem to me as believable as any alternative. Any theory about the afterlife will remain unproven. We will never know what it is about until we get there. My beliefs, again, give me comfort, especially on the days I miss Zach and Kaya's physical presence intensely. The notion that all traces of us cease to exist when we die is too bleak an outlook for someone who has lost a loved one, and who is approaching physical death himself. As always, it comes down to choice, and I have made mine. It helps me grieve and cope with the challenges that have been forced upon me in this lifetime.

CHAPTER TWENTY

August 26, 2016

Happy 22nd Birthday Zach. Today is your 22nd birthday. Instead of celebration, we will be honoring you by going out as a family and enjoying your passion for good food. Hopefully we will be able to reflect on all of your great qualities and smile some of the time instead of feeling overwhelmed with sadness.

As you know I have been writing you birthday notes for a long time because my mortality has been tested for years with a terminal illness. The purpose was to leave you with a piece of me should I pass. Never did I think that you and Kaya would pass before me, but I guess that we can never really take anything for granted even if the probability of something occurring is very remote.

Everything that I know from that fateful February day was drawn to take you and Kaya to the river. You wouldn't have gone if it wasn't 15 degrees, sunny and beautiful. You wouldn't have gone if you didn't do the exact route the afternoon before with Ben and found the route serene, tranquil and safe. You wouldn't have gone if Kaya had gone to Cuba with you and your wonderful Guelph University friends. You wouldn't have gone if you weren't in the exact kayaks that Kaya had been raised in since she was 3. You wouldn't have gone if you weren't trained as a lifeguard. Finally, you wouldn't have gone if you hadn't found us our home on the water 9 months earlier. These are all the ironies that we have to come to terms with when facing your tragedies.

You both left us with no loose strings. Things were too conveniently left neatly tied up for this to have been just an accident. No feelings unexpressed, no words unsaid, no regrets for the past only sadness that you both won't be physically here in our present and futures. We now believe that on some level, unbeknownst to you both, your souls had learnt the lessons they needed to learn on Earth.

I always tell you in these letters, how proud I am of the man you are becoming, things to work on and how I only want you to be happy. I have now found that these same sentiments continue even though we no longer have you in the physical world. There are no lessons to offer you this year because I know that either you, or Kaya, or both of you have given the ultimate lesson to us; sacrificing your lives with the hope to save the one you love. That is a lesson that we would all like to believe that we would rise to for each other but, when push comes to shove, I don't know how many of us would do the same. You are both heroes and victims at the same time and because of this we your families have to be heroic in how we choose to live out the remainder of our lives even though it would be so much easier to be victims and hide away from our circumstances. You continue to push me even in the afterlife to be a better person and endure despite what many would think, Why bother?

I don't know if this part of my journey will be short or long, but I do know that I have to take the first step and not waste the precious time that I may have left. My goals will be to help Ben, Nathaniel and your Mom find some happiness again even if this is not as joyous as it once was. I will also work to have your ideals of love, loyalty, friendship, integrity and responsibility come to the forefront in those who you have touched and in those who you have yet to touch. Your smile, eye contact, handshake, hugs and your Gift

*to make everyone feel noticed and that they were important will be
remembered and cherished by all.*
   Happy Birthday Zach!
   Love you, now and forever,
   Dad

The theme of this birthday letter, of course, is all the little things
that had to occur for them to go out on the river on the day of the
accident. These are some of my what-ifs. I add to these my own
personal what-if: what if I had elected to not have a ventilator and
had died eighteen months before the accident. Could my death have
prevented Zach and Kaya's physical deaths?

I will never absolutely know this answer until I pass over. I believe
that anything that occurs in the present can change the fabric of the
future. I have come to believe in "predetermined lives" with multiple
possible "exit points." I have thought about how free choice could
exist within a predetermined life and how miracles from the divine
could occur. I can't reconcile every condition of human loss within
my beliefs, as some things are beyond the scope of our abilities.

I believe that everyone has a predetermined life with multiple
exit points when a soul can decide if it has accomplished what it
came here to learn and it can return to the Divine. The predetermined "map of life" is set on the other side. Free choice of a soul is
exercised throughout its physical life and influences qualities such
as hope, optimism, and the ability to recognize miracles. I believe
there are "prepackaged" miracles in everyone's life. They are like
billboards and road signs you see on a highway. If you are aware,
engaged, and optimistic, you are more likely to read the signs and
billboards and choose a different path. If you are sleepy, unengaged
with physical life, in despair, you are less likely to see the miracles
in your life. Sometimes the messages on the billboards tell our souls
that the time is right for an exit. Life purposes have been fulfilled, it

is time to return to divinity. Other times, the signs reveal miracles that help our spirits grow and stay in the physical form, as there is more to fulfill. And still other times, the soul becomes despondent with physical life and is unable to see miracles that might keep the soul in physical form. It wants to return home even if it has not fulfilled its purposes. Ultimately free choice of the soul decides the time when we will join the Divine.

These beliefs give me comfort when dealing with the tragedies within my life. I know that beliefs aren't "truths" but there will never be absolute "truths" for these questions while we are in the physical form.

CHAPTER TWENTY-ONE

The Living

THE LAST THING OUR lost loved ones want is for us to forget our loved ones who are still among us. And with this book focusing so much on myself and the passing of Zach and Kaya it might appear that I am fixated on my losses. Despite my grief, however, I have remained very much in physical life. I live for my family, Darlene, Zach, Ben, Nathaniel, and myself, and I am thankful that we continue to be resilient despite the cruelty of the tragedies we have been dealt.

Ben, who is studying construction engineering, has become the doer of the family. After taking two years away from school to heal, and while continuing in a loving relationship with his girlfriend, Savannah, he has managed the caretaking of our house and property. With his work colleagues, he has accomplished many of the finishing touches in our new home, including the man cave, which is meticulously true to Zach's vision for it. I believe that Ben will always have a close bond to this house because much of his healing has been done here. He has become more spiritual, compassionate, and outwardly loving, the one in his groups of friends and coworkers that people are drawn to for advice and support when they are confronted with adversity. Recently Eion, one of his close friends, passed at the age of twenty-one after a year of fighting acute leukemia. Eion was a remarkable young man and an old soul. When he was told that there was no further treatment for him and that he was going to pass, his first priority was to let all of his friends know individually and in small groups that he was at peace with his fate. Ben was one of the first friends to know and he helped Eion fulfill this gift to his friends. Darlene and I were proud of how he supported Eion and their friends throughout this horrific yet loving experience.

Losing Zach and Kaya had also severely disrupted Nathaniel's life and plans. After the shock had passed, he was able to continue some traveling with his then-girlfriend, Erica. First, a safe trip across Canada, getting to know their own country better. After that, a trip to Bali, an island known for its spirituality and healing, and later to Thailand. Nathaniel is now in Halifax, where he has found a nice balance between university work and playtime. He, too, is growing beyond our family tragedy and has become more thoughtful and caring. It has enhanced his spirituality and he has come to under-stand the importance of meditation in one's life. He recently found a beautiful gray-blue feather from one of the blue herons that fish the river behind our house. The feather symbolizes patience, grace, and confidence. These are all qualities I would use to describe Nathaniel.

What becomes of a mother who has lost something that was so much a part of her? In Darlene's case, she has made the choice to grow from the experience. Always a doer, she has devoted time to finding a spiritual path through the destruction. She is keeping communication with her three sons at the forefront because that is what they all need to adjust to their new realities. She is a loving and caring soul to all of us. Her perspective and focus on the truly important things in life help us all.

On a day of sadness near what would have been Zach's twenty-third birthday, Darlene and I were talking about our futures. We feel that we would like to help others who have experienced great loss. We believe we can authentically do this because we have survived great loss. Our discussion started with us thinking about how a retired physician who was adept at counseling could counsel after a nine-year absence, and ended with discussing that our path to helping others would be through the active route of coaching and that Darlene would take the lead in this for us. She went back to school, taking a four-hundred-hour program to help her attain her life coach certification. With her previous two degrees, her life experiences, and her compassionate nature, she has become an excellent coach. I will be the second fiddle in this endeavor, a role I am very happy to be playing.

I made sure to include my own well-being in my family. In my current state of mind without body I have particularly questioned what my purpose is. I used to say that I was only here for my family; now I know it was selfish of me to be selfless. I have discovered that I need a purpose (or maybe purposes) larger than my family's well-being to lead me through the rest of my time in the physical. Right now one of my purposes is writing this story. I hope it will encourage hope in others.

I remember, from the time of the accident, both of our families being cognizant of the need to limit the tragedy. We made sure that we were not so racked by grief as parents that we could not provide love and support to those left behind. Creating an environment that focused concurrently on our healing, and the boys' healing, was our goal. We had heard of other parents who did not do this, and the tragedies they had been through were perpetuated and fractured their families. Three years into our healing journey, it appears as though our path has been the right path. The cycle of grief will still come and go but we are no longer paralyzed in grief. We take the sadness as it comes, acknowledge it, and then use our new beliefs to comfort us and guide us away from fear and loss toward strength and togetherness.

* * *

Forgiveness is said to be one of the keys to true happiness. When I was younger, it was easy. I readily forgave little disputes among family and friends. At the same time, I was aware of old family grudges involving my grandmother and grandfather, tensions that were felt for two generations and in which forgiveness was never achieved. I thought those grudges belonged to other people. I never imagined that I would be in a situation of family strife and estrangement but here I am, joined by my younger brother, both of us estranged from our oldest sibling and maintaining an awkward relationship with our parents as a result of this decision.

It is partially my fault that this has occurred. Although unwillingly, I brought disease and unfathomable loss into our family and it has proven too much for some people to handle. Now I find myself in the position of knowing that it is best for me to forgive but not knowing how to do it. Can I forgive someone who feels they have done no wrong? Can I forgive someone who continues in the same patterns of behavior that hurt me or my nuclear family?

I have done a lot of work on this. I have written to the people with whom I feel an ongoing relationship is important. I have expressed my hurt about my older brother's lack of support for me and my family, and over my parents' failure to understand why we chose to be estranged from him, and I have asked for a meaningful apology with a path to prevent more hurt from occurring. These writings were met with defensiveness and without apology. Clearing the air and seeking reconciliation did not work. Maybe I have judged and shamed too much. I am learning that other people's behaviors are not for me to judge, yet still I feel abandoned. Is feeling hurt by the actions of others in itself enough to expect an apology?

I'm fortunate that I've only lost a few relationships over the course of my physical losses. Some were peripheral relationships I expected to exit our lives. People do change over time, interests change over time. I do not have to forgive because drifting apart is part of life. Nothing malicious has occurred. Central relationships are much more difficult to lose without a sense of abandonment. It is the abandonment that hurts me and my nuclear family. Yet from the perspective of those who have left, I might be seen as the one who abandoned the relationship. I upset the balance when I became ill. I asked for a change of behavior and when it did not occur, I asked for the estrangement to protect myself and my family from further rejection. So am I the one who should apologize for asking too much of people? Too much only because they were incapable of dealing with significant loss? As I am physically disabled against my will, maybe they are unable to cope, or to be empathetic, not by choice but because of who they are.

It is unreasonable to think only of how you would react if the roles were reversed because we each have different tolerances and skill sets. Maybe forgiveness becomes easier if we believe we are each born with limited, predetermined abilities. It has to be easier to forgive someone who has no control over how they behave. By thinking this way, however, free will is extinguished. Choice is eliminated, and that does not feel right to me. If I believe that my soul can grow through my choices when I'm faced with adversity, the same ability must be given to all of us. Some of us might not be given the genetic tools to come as easily to what I may see as the kindest path of action, but we all have the freedom to make that decision. Everyone chooses his or her priorities in life.

I have tried to conceptualize forgiveness in other ways. Maybe the people who have left my life did so because they were only meant to be in my life for a time, no matter how central they were to me then. How can I feel abandoned when that was only the time they were supposed to be available to me?

Yet the more I think about forgiveness, the more I realize it is a circular path: it always leads back to one's self. An act of forgiveness is not performed to help the person who committed the hurt. It is done to help the person who has suffered the hurt. By forgiving, we discharge the toxins of anger and resentment that linger in our psyches. We release the power the person had over us. For these reasons, I think we can forgive people without actually saying, *I forgive you*. This eliminates the potential of the retort, *I have done nothing to warrant your forgiveness*, a statement that will only intensify anger and resentment.

I believe most people who know the fragility of life are able to more readily ask for and give forgiveness. They do not view it, as do many others, as a sign of weakness or capitulation. They are more like children, able to approach life without judgment and with innate kindness for themselves and others. Maybe the real path to forgiveness is trying to reach back and learn from our younger selves. Ultimately, it is up to each of us to exercise our powers of forgiveness with the recognition that we ourselves benefit most when we forgive ourselves and, in whatever way we feel fits the circumstances, others. Forgiveness does not mean you have to rebuild relations; it means you remove the power the relationship had over you, whether or not it was recognized by the other party. Once this is done, you can focus on positive emotions. I have forgiven everyone who has hurt me in the past. This has helped me rid my body of the poison of resentment and move forward in my life.

No matter how hard you try to avoid it, forgiveness will be a part of your healing because it is ultimately a gift to yourself.

CHAPTER TWENTY-TWO

The Good Life (1)

I HAVE A MANTRA THAT I chant in my head before I face each morning. It consists of eighteen words, arranged alphabetically: "Abundance, balance, compassion, courage, empathy, faith, forgiveness, gratitude, hope, imperfection, integrity, joy, love, mindfulness, passion, peace, purpose, resilience." To me, these are the essential elements of a life well-lived.

Over time, as I have repeated the words in my daily ritual, I have come to appreciate that they are also necessary for resilience after profound loss. It is not a coincidence that the list ends at *resilience*. Each element is an integral part of resilience, and together the elements lead to resilience. If we strengthen these qualities within us, we will all live more happily in our imperfect lives. We will create the motion and personal growth required to overcome the many obstacles we encounter along the way.

We often think of *abundance* as meaning the possession of many material things. My definition of abundance is the possession of many of the qualities in this list and the resources and services necessary for us to overcome our obstacles. Most of us will have abundance in some facets of our lives but not in others. I feel that one of our purposes in life is to fill the gaps, to welcome into existence the qualities we are lacking, or to find peace in our lives without that quality. Also, I have learned that an abundance of resources, materially (so that your basic needs are covered), of positive personality traits, of family and friends, and of community in the form of affordable services and supportive programs to help strengthen our mental health and well-being, are essential for resilience.

Balance was not a quality that came to me right away. At times in my life, I spent too much time at work, which is easy to do when work is a calling for you. This caused friction at home and made me feel guilty for not prioritizing my young family. Before this reached a crisis, Darlene and I talked frankly about it and I adjusted my priorities, putting my family at the top where it belonged. Most human vices are only vices because they are taken to an extreme. The maxim "everything in moderation" counsels us to avoid pursuing our obsessions to the neglect of other equally important parts of our lives. Balance is a skill that can be attained with regular reflection. It is also required in managing grief. Profound loss and constant grief are exhausting. You need occasional distractions and to spend time on personal growth. Balance in your mourning allows you to experience the first sparks of hope from which you can see your new life going forward.

I define *compassion* as the ability to see suffering in others and doing something to help alleviate it. Suffering is all around us but if we stay in our own little worlds we can insulate ourselves from it. It also can be so prevalent in the world that we become overwhelmed and fail to respond to people in need. Any attempt, small or large, to alleviate suffering will have a positive effect on those around us. And compassion toward oneself will lessen the guilt a survivor feels for still being alive. Compassion to oneself is also necessary for resilience.

Courage helps us adapt to adversity. It allowed Zach and Kaya to choose to try to save each other. Courage has also kept us from giving up despite our immense adversities. Without courage, we would be victims of our tragedies. We need courage to help us ask for the help of others, laugh again and find joy in our lives.

Empathy is a cousin of compassion. When we have empathy, we are able to withhold judgment, putting ourselves in the shoes of others and seeing the world from their vantage points. Empathy can be developed and learned so there is hope for all of us to nurture and strengthen these skills. Doing so brings more peace to our lives because we better understand each other. Sometimes the differentiation between when we are acting because of compassion or because of empathy is difficult to understand. I believe I can only be empathetic when I have experienced a similar situation to that of the person I am trying to understand by viewing life from their perspective. For those whose experiences are not relatable for me, I don't have the ability to view their problem from their perspective but I can offer them my compassion. In my mind, the differences between when we are acting because of compassion or empathy are not important because the actions that either elicits are powerfully positive. Empathy is also a starting point for forgiveness, and being able to forgive others is another way to enhance peace of mind.

I have already discussed my *faith* and my thoughts on *forgiveness* which have been necessary to my resilience. One more thought about *faith*: If you aren't able to find a particular faith in which to believe, having faith In the sole fact that things will get better will help you during the most trying times.

I wrestle with *gratitude*. How can I be grateful for the last twelve years of my life, given everything that has happened? It would be insane to be grateful for all I have lost so I concentrate instead on the individual growth I have attained, and seen others attain as a result of our experiences. Life with ALS has taught me patience and has shown me that I can live without physical pleasure. The physical loss of Zach and Kaya has taught me the importance of love and of our spiritual existence. I would have done anything to avoid our tragedies but I believe that Darlene and the boys will now be better able to manage their grief at my eventual physical death because of all that has transpired. The grief work that we have done will give them the perspective to go on without my physical being. I am grateful for this.

Also, the truth is that on most days I feel fortunate for what I have and do not think about what I lack. I live pain-free in an environment where I actively contribute to the well-being of the people I love. I give love and receive it from family and friends, most of all from my wife, Darlene, and my sons. Despite ALS, my boys still remember a healthy, active, physically fit father. I am not defined by them as helpless and dependent. I have lived longer than most with ALS and because of this I have been able to leave my loved ones some legacy, including these writings. Each of my family members has been greatly challenged by life but is still able to love and find joy. I have been able to add lifelong friendships during every phase of my life and have lived in a community that continues to support me and my family. For this, too, I am grateful. I have learned that when you reflect on your life's circumstances you can always find something for which to feel gratitude, and those feelings promote acceptance, relieve suffering, and counteract despair. Gratitude takes you from being a victim to being a survivor.

Hope is essential for a good life. It fuels our dreams and aspirations. As a physician, I was often amazed at how some people with terminal illnesses managed to hold on to hope. Now that I have a terminal illness myself, I understand how this is possible, although hope for me is complicated, much like gratitude. In the aftermath of loss, hope disappears and takes its time returning. And now, while I can hope for better things for my family, knowing that Darlene and the boys have the strength to activate that hope now and in the future, it can be difficult to sustain individual hope while living with a terminal illness. Yet most days I fill my time with productive activities and find things to look forward to. I hope that I am still able to give myself personal challenges and continue to have my purposes unfold in my everyday life. I hope that someday I can have greater personal abilities than I now enjoy.

Imperfection is part of being human. I have seen so many people strive for unrealistic goals of perfection, and even though some are able to find short-lived perfection in one aspect of their lives, it is usually at the expense of something else. This seems especially a problem for young people today. They have anxiety about being anything less than perfect, some of it ingrained in their own personalities, some of it as a result of pressure from their families and society. They fear failure, which they measure as anything less than perfection. I have been a high achiever in life and I know the pressure to be perfect. Still, I had the chance, while young, to succeed by being imperfect, to learn from my mistakes, which are far better teachers than our accomplishments. I had many avenues open to me and I did not have to compete at such an early age for academic and athletic accomplishment.

I have become much better acquainted with imperfection over the last twelve years, and it has taught me what is truly important to a good life. I have gained perspective, which can only come to us from imperfection. When everything in life is going well, we have no need to wonder why we are happy. Pondering existential questions is something most of us need to be pushed toward. It has not been an easy path but rarely do great achievements come without great work. I have made peace with my imperfection.

Integrity is a small word that encompasses much. It is our honesty, our ability to take responsibility for our mistakes and to show kindness and empathy to others. It is about using the right words and taking the right actions. It is patience, calmness, inclusiveness, and humility. Integrity is being congruent with the divinity within us all. It is also necessary for self-respect, which in turn enables self-love, and it is only through loving ourselves that we foster resilience.

Joy is happiness on steroids. It is the emotion that has the highest vibration and as such, it brings us closest to divinity. During the last twelve years, I have lived with too much sadness. I knew joy before, and I know I have to find joy again because it is the frequency of being that brings me closest to my true self. I doubt that I will be able to attain *pure* joy, given our losses, but I hope I can find something close to it. And if I can entertain the possibility of joy in my life, I hope that others will be able to experience it in the simple fact of being able.

Love is the sun that nurtures, strengthens, and enables us to grow physically and spiritually. It transcends time, distance, even life and death. Love can connect us all and eventually will connect us all. Love keeps us fighting the obstacles in our lives. We must love ourselves before we can share this gift with others. Unconditional love is the greatest gift we can give or receive.

In a world of increasing distractions, *mindfulness* is a lost practice. The principles are simply being in the "now" and taking the time to acknowledge the "now" in a nonjudgmental manner. Shaking off distractions, you recognize the peace of stillness. You escape comparisons of your past to your present, and of your present to some imagined future. I believe that being mindful and practicing mindfulness through regular meditation can bring us all out of darkness and help us defeat many of the world's woes as well as our individual woes.

Passion puts love into action. It puts our hearts into our activities and puts action into our life's purposes. It transforms our activities into callings and is the kindling of great deeds. It brings two people together and makes them one. It reignites the enthusiasm for life that is blown out after significant loss. Continued passion for life is necessary for a resilient life.

Peace is the state we obtain when we stop frantically grasping for more or better. We appreciate the good in our lives and no longer need to have more. I have come to peace with ALS and I am not actively looking for a cure. If a cure does come within my lifetime, I will be joyous. I am not waiting for it to happen. I will live the life I have been given to the best of my ability. I do not know if I will find peace in every aspect of my life, particularly with regard to the loss of Zach and Kaya. But I have faith that when I join their souls I will find peace with every loss I have had in my physical life.

I once believed that we were given life to fulfill a greater *purpose*. I have now come to believe that purpose unfolds in every circumstance and stage of our lives. If we remain open, we will have and fulfill many purposes in our lives. If we believe that we are here for only one reason, we will not take the many other opportunities that present themselves for individual growth. My purposes have included being a good father, a loving and supportive husband, serving others as a physician, being a mentor in medicine and a coach in sports, being an inspiration to others by demonstrating perseverance and resilience after great personal loss. I know I have fulfilled many other purposes, some known to me and some not. Allowing purposes to continue to unfold in my life gives me the ability to continually renew myself and allows me to be defined by something other than my disabilities.

Resilience, finally, is the ability to persevere and flourish in the face of real adversity. Everyone faces adversity, whether it be through divorce, grief, health problems, or job loss. I define real adversity as that which forces you to redefine your future. Resilience is not simply moving on with life after something occurs. It can only come through incorporating loss into one's life through personal growth. Personal growth enables us to flourish in all aspects of life. I believe that ALS made me a stronger person. It taught me skills that would prove invaluable as I faced the tragedy of Zach and Kaya, enabling me to adjust my emotions and adapt my spiritual beliefs and find a path forward.

Adding resilience to the aforementioned qualities allows one to live a good life.

CHAPTER TWENTY-THREE

The Good Life (2)

I N MY CAPACITY AS A father to three boys, I have another set of values, consistent with the ones discussed in the previous chapter, that I like to share with them in conversation and in the letters I write. Some of these relate to character, some to the physical world, some to the spiritual, and still others to the pleasures of life. Together, they amount to another formula for personal growth and a life well-lived.

The first thing I advise them is be honest. I have found that one of the most important qualities in the colleagues I worked with was their trustworthiness. Far too often, I found people would tell little white lies to cover up for something they did or failed to do, and because of this they could not be trusted. It did not matter how smart they were. They developed reputations for lacking integrity. Unfortunately, when an adult is caught in a lie it is difficult for him or her to regain his or her reputation. The lesson is to always be honest in your dealings: your reputation is hard to establish and one lie can ruin it no matter how honest you have been in the past or may be in the future.

Some of us are born with confidence and others acquire it. Regardless of how it comes, it needs to be nurtured throughout a person's life. My son Zach was born with this trait. From a young age, he could talk to adults as a peer. Practically everything he tried he found success in. Being a gifted athlete seemed to reinforce his sense of self. By contrast, my son Ben, like me, was shy when young and afraid of standing out in a crowd. Public speaking was a particular challenge for both of us, culminating with each of us fainting during public speaking presentations in elementary school.

I began to figure out how to manage my shyness in grade ten Biology when I had to give a twenty-minute class presentation. To counteract my fears, I put a lot of work into the preparation of my topic. I came off well and I learned a valuable lesson from that experience. Preparation can be an antidote to the fear of public speaking. In short, I was learning to nurture my self-confidence. Ben did the same at a similar period of his life and is now a very confident young man. Confidence starts with thinking that you can do whatever you put your mind to, and it grows with each little success we experience. It will be challenged with failure, but failure also gives us the opportunity to learn and improve. Challenging our personal fears and putting the work into making ourselves better promotes true inner strength and self-confidence.

I should add that optimism can be nurtured in a similar way. There will be obstacles in your life that thwart your dreams and aspirations. Some of these will hit early, and some later in life. Whenever they come, they will be unexpected and they will undermine your hopes for a better tomorrow. If you remain optimistic, you can survive the chaos that obstacles create. You can train yourself to stay your course, to cope with and navigate your obstacles, and still find within you the power to give to the people around you. You might have to adjust or change your hopes. Regardless of whether they are big or small, realistic or ambitious, the important thing is that you have them.

There will always be terrible days and longer periods of time when you go to dark places. These times can be awfully frustrating.

We tend to dwell on them, overthink them, and lose sight of the fact that they are neither permanent nor a true reflection of our reality. It is important to recognize them as dark days and remember that like most unpleasant things in life they will pass and we will return to normal. We need simply to cope with them, knowing that the majority of our days will be better. (If your dark periods last for longer than a few weeks, I recommend that you see a health care professional so that they can assess if you could be clinical depressed, a common problem now with one in five people meeting the clinical guidelines of a major depressive disorder.)

When I was a Boy Scout, we would recite at the beginning of each of our meetings the Scouting Creed which includes the instruction, "Do a good deed every day." Once in a while, I would do things on my own initiative to make life easier for my parents. I probably give myself more credit than I deserve but I think I helped out, and I remember how much joy my parents took in these random acts of kindness, and how good I felt performing them. Scouting is not as popular as it used to be but a commitment to doing good deeds still has its benefits, especially when you consider that altruism gives both the giver and the receiver so much. In more recent times, the "Pay it Forward " campaign has stimulated the performance of countless selfless acts. Hopefully, the ethic behind it will flourish.

I have already expressed my thoughts on religion. I have found raising children in traditional Christian faiths to be difficult in our times because of historical wrongs, scientific challenges, various forms of intolerance, gender inequalities, and other issues. It is nevertheless an important part of a person's education to know something about all the major religions. I would like to learn more about Hinduism, Islam, Judaism, Buddhism, and the traditional teachings of Indigenous peoples. All have something to contribute to the moral foundations of civilization. I would advise all young people to look into these faiths and seize on whatever connects them to a larger spirit or purpose, remembering that religion should be inclusive rather than divisive.

Notwithstanding my comments on organized Christianity, I do think there is wisdom in the Ten Commandments, and one of particular importance to our time concerns false idols. Those of us in developed nations display a ridiculous reverence for the people who entertain us, whether in sports, music, or on-screen. We are celebrity obsessed. We follow every moment of our favorites' lives on Instagram, Twitter, and Facebook, and we imitate them by manipulating our own public images to seem more celebrity-like. We post photos, quotes, accomplishments, and milestones on the Internet to make us feel worthy. Rather than looking inward for self-love, we measure our success by how many "likes" we receive. We are trying to idolize ourselves as well as our celebrities, and often we wind up loathing ourselves for failing to meet the ridiculous standards set on social media. Cultivating humility is a surer route to real happiness.

Spiritual advisers can be helpful in negotiating life's challenges. I have several. One is my parish priest, who visits from time to time and engages me in discussions of free will, dream theory, religious history, and other issues I find fascinating. I have conversations with him that go places I haven't gone since I was in my teens and my friends would stay up late talking about big concepts and the meaning of life, solving all of humanity's problems by 3 a.m. Spiritual advisers come in many forms. They can be readings, friends, clergy, songwriters, people you barely know. The important thing is that you find significance and meaning in what they communicate. So often in life, we get overwhelmed with the mundane and fail to remain open to the spiritual side of ourselves. The work you do to keep your mind open to spiritual messages will always be rewarding.

Music is another way to lift your spirit. My life has been greatly affected by the music I have heard. I like almost every genre of music, as my eclectic music library will attest, although there is one band, Rush, that I have followed more closely than any other since I was thirteen when vinyl albums ruled the world. I would listen to Rush for hours upon hours, and I still do today. I've followed the band from LPs to cassette tapes to CDs and DVDs to digital formats, and I own all their albums. I always find something in their music that speaks to me personally. I can bring back certain periods of my life and remember what I was doing when I first heard a song. Each piece of music is a tiny time machine bringing me back to my past. So pick a band (or an artist) and listen to its work in its entirety. I have found that the "greatest hits" of any band only gives you a superficial look into their work. The treasures are revealed upon deeper scrutiny. This will take you on a journey of discovery, one that will lift your heart, bring you energy, and enrich your life in unexpected ways.

* * *

Our first color television came when I was eight. There was only one TV in the house at that time. My first experience with computers was in middle school. The school had three Commodore PETs, available only to kids in the accelerated classes, which was horribly elitist. Fortunately, I had some smart friends and was able to get into the dark little room in which the PETs were housed. I also had a grade eight English teacher who was a futurist, constantly telling us that computers would soon be in everyone's home and a part of our everyday lives. My parents were early adopters and I was in grade nine when we got a Radio Shack TRS-80, 4K color computer. Unfortunately, we didn't learn much from it except how to play games. Several decades later, things have developed more quickly than even my teacher predicted. Counting tablets, smartphones, smart TVs, laptops, and desktops, we have eleven computers in our house, all doing something important for someone living here.

I readily admit the benefits of this technology. Without it, I would scarcely be able to communicate with my family. But I can't help but feel we are losing things as a result of our endless screen time.

When I first became a physician, we used pagers and then "unsmart" cell phones to keep us connected to the hospital. We were often urgently needed. Now everyone is tied to the office around the clock by smartphones, not because of life-and-death situations, but simply because it is possible. Nothing in life is so sacred that it cannot be interrupted by a ringtone or a vibration. We have been trained to respond immediately to our screens. This might be excusable if the communications were essential but unfortunately, the majority are unimportant Facebook updates from people we would never bother to meet face-to-face, tweets of inconsequential events, and spam from hustlers. We have slowly lost our ability to sit still and enjoy the quiet. My advice is to go offline every now and then. Turn off the screen. There is peace in being unavailable.

On a similar note, find time to relax. Routines are fine but sometimes we get so deep into them and feel we need to have everything perfect before we can sit down and put our feet up. Some Type A people never relax because there is always something to do, some other project to be tackled. We are forever chasing our tails to the detriment of our physical and mental health. If you're this way, or if you're merely overwhelmed from time to time, step back and think about how many of your best memories involve constant work. Recognize the fact that you need to take time for yourself and play as hard as you work.

Some of the strongest memories I have of peacefulness and tranquility involve the sounds of nature. When I take the time to listen, they still give me comfort. I know no better sound than leaves rustling in the wind. The best time to hear them is in late summer as the crisper winds blow in. Other sounds such as the bubbling of a spring brook energize me immediately. I love the sound of rain on a roof, especially when it is pouring in buckets from the heavens, and the power and intensity of crickets singing in unison, so intense that your ears can hardly take it and then it stops as quickly as it started. Sound envelops you in the moment. The best place to hear all these sounds is away from the city, so make sure that you spend some time each year out-of-doors, with all your media turned off, listening to the wonders of nature.

It goes without saying that part of enjoying nature is caring for nature. There is an episode in the popular TV drama, *Mad Men,* in which the Draper family is out for a family picnic, relaxing on a blanket after a big lunch. When it's time for them to leave, Don shakes the garbage off his blanket, all the cardboard, waxed paper, and glass bottles, and leaves it on the ground. This scene, circa 1960, would be unthinkable now, although I can remember as a kid dropping soda cans and candy wrappers on the ground when I was done with them. I would not even think about it. It was around this time that we first saw those novel advertisements with an owl saying, *Give a hoot! Don't pollute.* The obscene littering and pollution of the post-war years is slowly but surely coming under control although there are still serious problems, including our acceptance and support of the plastic packaging derived from oil products. Public pressure can change these norms. Some of us remember when most McDonald's burgers came in Styrofoam packaging. Suddenly someone woke us up and public pressure put an end to it. The same is happening now with plastic grocery bags, straws, and other single-use plastic items. We need to be conscious of the waste and nonbiodegradable stuff we leave behind.

And while you're outside, or even inside, find occasions to challenge yourself physically. When I reflect on my accomplishments in life, I find that some of the best feelings come from physical challenges I have overcome. They mark my life like a time signature on a music sheet. I remember twenty-mile hikes with heavy backpacks that we had to perform in Scouts, and my first ten-kilometer run in high school, and my last ten-kilometer run before I was diagnosed with ALS. These are not great distances compared to some people's accomplishments but they are accomplishments all the same, and by reaching my goals I felt satisfied and proud of myself. I know Darlene feels the same way about her half marathons. These were run at a time when she needed accomplishments attributable solely to her determination. The successful completion of a physical challenge does great things for your sense of well-being, and we all need jolts to our self-esteem now and then.

* * *

We are all so busy with our lives, trying to pack in as many experiences as we can, that we can lose track of time. That's a good reason to pay attention to the milestones. A big one for me was the day Zach left for university. We were able to visit the campus and help move him into his room. For me, it was bittersweet. I could not go into his residence as it was not accessible. Nor could I help lug his bar fridge up to his room. I did tour the campus with him and our family and got a feel for the place where he would spend the next four years of his life. I could feel all the exciting opportunities before him, and I was able to appreciate and acknowledge that milestone. I have seen most of my children's milestones and I recall them with great fondness. Milestones are a great way of maintaining perspective on your life, and the lives of your loved ones.

Another way of keeping track of time is to protect your nostalgic places. There are certain corners of the world that return us to positive moments from our pasts. They might have been neglected through the years, or they might have changed substantially, but to those who knew them when, they will still bring feelings of warmth and excitement. (Certain objects can do the same. They may look to others like crappy old stuff, relics from a bygone era, but to those who understand their significance they can be a direct line to childhood enthusiasms, they will someday want to share with their own children.) I have accumulated many nostalgic places over the years, some of which were passed to me by my parents, others I found for myself. I hope to help my children find similar places they will want to cherish and share with their children someday. Some they will remember for their own reasons, perhaps a secret first for them that I will never know about (and that is fine with me). The important thing is that they have them.

To the same end, I have recorded stories from my childhood that I share with my boys. They help explain how I became the person I am, and children are always interested in tales of what it was like to grow up at a different time. My dad has started to do this recently and as a result of his writings, I know so much more than I did know about him. My illness has given me the time to record parts of my story, and it has also lent me a sense of urgency in getting things down. Terminal illness impresses upon you that time is finite for a human vessel. So write out your childhood memories while you still have them. Composing them will give you as much pleasure as sharing them.

While you're at it, write a letter to the special people in your life. I have mentioned that when I was diagnosed with my illness I started writing letters to my sons and my wife on birthdays, anniversaries, at Christmas, and so on. They give me the opportunity to tell my loved ones that they are admired and unconditionally loved. I am also able to share stories and some fatherly advice to help them in their journeys. I should have done this earlier. Prior to my illness, I would get the appropriate card, add a few sentences, and that would be it. The letters I write now say so much more, and they can be kept forever and shared with my grandchildren, who will know me better through these pages than by any other means. Writing letters to loved ones is a way each of us can be a little bit immortal, and letters will make the lives of their recipients a little easier when we are no longer physically present for them.

Sharing your thoughts and feelings directly with others is a way of fostering emotional intelligence. We are all born with an intellectual quotient (IQ) that stays relatively stable through our lives, barring traumatic head injuries or dementia. This may seem unfair to those of us not in the gifted category, but just because you are not among the intellectual elite does not mean you cannot improve your emotional quotient. It is also important to our success in life. IQ may get you through the door but EQ ultimately decides whether or not you will move in an organization, and EQ can grow over time if we pay attention to our experiences. EQ measures our skills of compassion, empathy, our ability to give and receive love, and our ability to delay gratification. High EQs are common in youth who have had profound loss. I will bet that the people you admire most have a high EQ. They are leaders because they practice the skills of emotional intelligence and have made upgrading these skills a lifelong mission.

Last but most important, when you find your partner in life, do not be afraid to truly love them. Loving has many components. It starts with providing support and trust and making their welfare a priority in your life. Your beloved should feel and have the inner knowledge that they are the most important person in your life! Physically, making love is all about deeply trusting your partner so that you can explore your sexuality. Having meaningless sex is nice for the moment but it pales in comparison to a real sexual encounter with your loved one. Don't be afraid to push boundaries because if you don't you'll find that your sex life will suffer from boredom. Talk about your needs and wants and even your fantasies with your partner; once this is all out there you will become closer as a couple. Listen to and respect your partner's wishes and limitations and you'll find that in this environment things will mature with time. Nothing beats two lovers linked to each other in the ultimate expression of caring, respect, and love.

A true, loving relationship allows each person to grow, thrive, and flourish.

CHAPTER TWENTY-FOUR

In the End

I AM STILL DEBILITATED by ALS but I no longer feel that I am defined by my body. I feel somewhat like a soul without any of the physical pleasures of man. I live in my mind a lot, reflecting on why, despite an imperfect life, I feel as though it has been a good life.

I have learned that happiness is not something we find; it is something we must nurture from within. I continue to cultivate happiness, knowing that my physical life can go at any time. My pleasure comes from helping my family and others thrive through love. I mentioned earlier my wish that my children would have happy lives. I know now that setbacks and despair are necessary ingredients for a happy life. We can only be truly grateful for living if we have felt despair.

I think also about life's purpose. The answer may be as simple as living with a sense of kindness to other people and to all other manifestations of life. I am convinced that we all choose how our purposes will be directed. We might be family directed, as Darlene has been in her life, selflessly sacrificing personal needs for the needs of my disabilities and for her sons. We might be community directed, as I was during my medical practice and am continuing to be in my advocacy for ALS, or nationally directed, as I have been in my support for medical assistance in dying, for the terminally ill. Our purposes in life will ultimately unfold effortlessly because they are ingrained in us.

I know that I lived an unexamined life until the unexpected loss of Zach and Kaya. I would have gladly kept living an unexamined life if that would have kept them with us longer. Some things we do not get to choose. Disease and death surround us. Some people evade extreme loss until they are old. Some, like me, face it in middle age, and some, like my boys, have had to face it from childhood. We do not choose what we face or when we face it but we do get to choose how we face it, and if we can meet it with resilience it will be beneficial to us. Resilience might not save our physical lives when we have a terminal disease, but it will certainly benefit ourselves and our loved ones if we are able to give and receive love despite the obstacles in our lives.

Would I have chosen a different path? Of course. If I was given the opportunity, I would have continued on my path of helping people in my community. That was my original purpose. I would rather that ALS and the loss of Zach and Kaya had not entered our lives, but these were circumstances beyond control. I have made what I could of my horrendous losses and I trust that I have become a better person, that we all have become better people, through our losses.

We are continually learning to be less judgmental and more empathetic. We appreciate the gifts that Zach and Kaya have brought into our lives from the other side, the greatest being faith in the immortality of life and the knowledge that we are now and will forever be together.

When I dream about passing, it no longer fills me with dread. I remember being afraid of death when I was young, not because I thought consciousness failed to exist in the afterlife but because it did exist. I felt sad picturing myself alone, watching life go on without me for eternity. This fear left me in my early twenties when we all feel invincible. Upon my diagnosis, I was not scared of death so much as anxious to be alive for Darlene and our sons. Now I have accepted my inevitable death and I await it with curiosity. I do not know when I will physically die but I do know that when it happens it will be as it is supposed to be. I have surrendered myself to the universe. By surrendering, I do not mean that I have given up on physical life. I have simply decided to go with the flow of life and let it lead me to whatever is next, whether the opportunity is in the physical dimension or the spiritual dimension. I trust that the universe is trying to do the best for the divinity inside all of my family. Regardless of what befalls me, there will be no guilt or regrets among those I inevitably leave behind.

I hope that my death will not come too late for Darlene. The past twelve years have certainly taken their toll. I have begun to wonder if I can be more helpful to my family from the other side than I am here, and more and more I question where I would prefer to be, cognizant of how limiting my earthly presence is for Darlene and myself. When I hear about friends meeting and traveling on special occasions, it brings me sadness because Darlene deserves to be living that life. She deserves to be living that life with me, but with that option taken away, what is the next best for us all? Despite my doubts, Darlene tells me that I am still the "love of her life" and the "pillar of her strength." She chooses to be with me through love and does not want to think of a time when we will not be physically together.

* * *

A terminal disease forces you to think about how you will be remembered. As I reflect on my life, I know I want people to remember me as I once was, healthy, strong, and vibrant. I do not want to be reduced to the guy in the chair who can only talk with his eyes. I do not want my disease to define who I am or who I was here on earth. I know it will, but I would prefer people to remember what else I was.

I open my eyes and un-cup my ears, and suddenly the world comes alive with a brilliant noon sun and the deafening ringing of crickets. I have walked a long way from my regular world to a picnic on the other side of the brook. I run to escape a dragonfly that has been skimming the surface of the pond. I am afraid of this beautiful creature, thinking it will use its black tail to stitch me as if I was getting sutures in the emergency room. Will you remember this me?

"Red rover, red rover, we call Jeff over." Gleefully, I charge into the human chain, the linked arms of my friends. With speed and strength, I break the chain and recruit more kids to my team. Recesses are filled with running games. The faster you run, the sooner you're picked for a team. I'm near the top of everyone's selection. Stocky, sturdy, agile, I run my best in every game except for the "chase and kiss" game that erupts every spring. In this game, I was never as fast as the girls. Will you remember this me?

The slap of the ball stings my hand as I play catch with my dad. I pick up the smell of burning charcoal as the electric lighter coil ignites the hibachi barbecue. My dad hollers with delight as he delivers another perfectly placed pitch. Together, as a family, we sit around our new brown picnic table and enjoy hamburgers complemented by Mom's homemade macaroni and potato salads. Afterward, we sit and watch the night fall, entertained by stories of the past. Will you remember this me?

The morning greets us with blue sky as we hastily cook our pancakes on the Coleman stove. Clouds surround us as we prepare for a long day of hiking and evaluation. Soon our fourteen-year-old bodies are struggling through the rain, our heavy gear soaked with water, doubling its weight. We soldier on and are rewarded with a top-ten finish, ahead of the honor squad in our Scout troop. Will you remember this me?

Standing alone, I look out over the empty field, knowing this could be my last game. I ask myself what I can do today to make me and my team better. I know it will be another day of hard hits, as we try to move the ball forward yard by yard, and I know I will hurt by the end of the game. During my three years of playing, I have come to love football. I walk back to the locker room with "Eye of the Tiger" blasting in my ears. Will you remember this me?

Waiting awkwardly at the front of the church, I catch the first glimpse of my bride-to-be. I am overwhelmed by her beauty and all my nerves are instantly calmed. We are united as one and we confidently stroll back down the aisle. We dance to our song with the comfort that you can only get between two people who are destined to be together forever. Will you remember this me?

I am in room number one as the siren approaches. I know there has been a horrific accident, but I do not yet know the severity of the injuries. A broken three-year-old boy is brought through the entrance. I summon all the ABCDEs of my trauma training and take the lead in pulling him back from near death. The team stabilizes this boy with bags of normal saline, chest tubes, and intubation. I accompany him by helicopter to the accepting pediatric unit. Pleased with the knowledge that we have done a fantastic job, I hand him off to the pediatric trauma surgeon. Will you remember this me?

Softly, I sing to my son gently rocking him to and fro. This is the reprieve I give to my exhausted wife who does the lion's share of the night work with our newborn baby who does not like to

sleep. After he has nodded off to my lullaby, we watch old movies played on our VCR. Cuddling on our blue leather recliner,
we intermittently fall to and from sleep as the first rays of a new
morning creep through the blinds. Will you remember this me?

The alarm rings in my ears, awakening me from much-
needed sleep on a cold January morning. I slip out of bed and
wake my son. We are fortunate to have the late game today,
meaning we're on the ice at seven fifteen a.m., him as a player,
me as his coach. After the game, we chow down on eggs, bacon,
hash browns, and rye toast. A reward for venturing from winter
to the ice on a January morning. Will you remember this me?

I stand defiantly at the podium and wonder to myself how a
shy, compliant boy has become a leader of a cause. For once in
my life, words flow eloquently from my mouth. We march on
the capitol building at Queen's Park chanting "Save our hospital!" We draw the attention of the health minister and beat back
our ruthless CEO who has tried to put an organization's needs
above a community's needs, rescuing our little hospital from
the ignominious fate of outpatient outpost. Blood has been
drawn and I am quietly dismissed from my hospital leadership
position. Will you remember this me?

Delicately, I pull a little harder, trying to keep the head and
shoulders perpendicular to each other. With a reassuring fetal
heart rate, I whisper encouragement: "One more push and she
is here!" And she arrives, wet and wailing. I clamp the cord in
two spots and put her on her anxious, exhausted mother. Proud
Father cuts the cord and we all smile. Will you remember this
me?

Together we walk hand in hand, as we have been doing since
the beginning. We walk in the sand and watch the waves behind
us remove all trace of our existence. That night we explore each
other not as a couple that has been together for twenty-three

years but as if we were meeting for the first time. My leg shakes excitedly, a return to adolescence. Our morning run through this island paradise invigorates us and we enjoy another day of sunshine and alone time. Will you remember this me?

Stubbornly, I stare forward with a face devoid of expression and a little drool on my chin. A soft wisp can be heard as the air is pushed into my lungs. My body is in full relaxation. My arms hang uselessly from my torso and I have developed a slightly rotund stomach. I have done some good even in this situation and I know as time passes this condition could last as long as my healthy time. I still cannot help but think that I am in the Fat Elvis stage of my life. Like him, I will be remembered for my condition late in life, as a man who needs instead of a man who does. Please don't remember just this me.

EPILOGUE

THIS BOOK HAS BEEN about change and the choices I
have made in my life when confronted with change. Most
of it was written in the first year following the physical loss of
Zach and Kaya. It was initially a way to help me deal with immense
pain. After I read through my writings, I felt the words could help
others deal with their adversities. Initially, I had written sparingly
about our experience with ALS, probably because I did not let myself
grieve my own physical losses and the losses that my family has
experienced as a result of living twelve years with this horrific disease.
From a superficial perspective, we sometimes make ALS look easy.
It is not easy and I decided to give readers a brutally frank look at
my internal thoughts and our daily life. The truth is that initially,
everyone hates what they become as a result of ALS. I felt this way
but I knew it was important for my family to see me coping well
with my circumstances. It has taken a while for me to make peace
with my situation and I can now honestly say that I am grateful to
be living a purposeful life.

This book depicts the struggles of my extended family in a deeply
personal way, not to shame anyone but because I think the reality
of how a family copes with tragedies is important knowledge for
others experiencing the disruption that follows adversity. If nothing
else, they know they are not alone. I love everyone in my family and
recognize that breakdowns happen and the fixing of relationships

is difficult because everyone feels like a victim, and to some extent we are all indeed victims of these tragedies. Despite the toll on my extended family, I am happy to say that my parents and I now have a good relationship. I am proud of them for managing the stress that estrangement has created by not playing favorites. My relative that blamed me following the accident has apologized and chosen to grow from the experience. I am hopeful that sometime in the future a true reconciliation may occur with my brother and his family.

The passing of Zach and Kaya has brought the Firths into our lives. We would all have preferred to have been in-laws but we have to acknowledge how our spiritual children have brought us together to help us grieve and mourn. This is not a likely scenario after tragedy and we are grateful for the relationship.

Resiliency is a legacy that we as parents of Kaya and Zach will continue to foster by creating scholarships for young people who choose resiliency in their lives following loss. Although in name it is a tribute to Zach and Kaya, it represents how proud we are of all our children for being resilient following the passing of their oldest siblings. This idea was planted by us but it has grown into much more through friends of Zach and Kaya and the creation of an annual golf fund-raising tournament for the scholarship fund. We are especially grateful to the Biehn family for this gift. The Zach Sutherland and Kaya Firth Resiliency Scholarship Fund has in only three years awarded over $20,000 to youth for postsecondary education. Through the website choose2beresilient.com, it has provided resources to help youth and families cope with grief and build resilience so that they can flourish. If you want to learn more about Zach and Kaya, please go to this website and you will find photos and descriptions of how they lived their lives. If you find our project to recognize resilient youth resonates with you, there is a donor page on this website. We look forward to growing this important initiative into the future.

Darlene has started coaching people, formally and informally. She is naturally gifted with the ability to help and care for people and is finally finding time to exist not only in a state of doing but of being. We're also coaching together and are enjoying helping others develop the best versions of themselves.

I have remained in good physical health despite living on a ventilator. I sometimes feel disingenuous for describing myself as living with a "terminal" disease because I am still here. I know I am very fortunate. So many people with ALS and other equally horrific diseases or life circumstances have not had the same fortune. I am grateful for the love and support I have received throughout my physical life. As for my legacy, I have come to believe that the greatest things we leave behind are the joyful memories our loved ones have of us when we were just being ourselves.

Finally, if my journey has piqued your interest in what it's like to have ALS, I offer you the Still Life Challenge. Undertake it with a responsible companion and an empty bladder.

The Still Life Challenge

1. Sit in a comfortable chair with all distractions turned off.

2. Have your responsible companion duct-tape your arms and legs to the chair.

3. Have your companion duct-tape your mouth (only if you are able to breathe comfortably through your nose).

4. Try to communicate with your companion by having them go through the alphabet with you blinking when the correct letter is reached to spell your word(s).

5. Try to do this for an hour.

6. Make a donation to your local ALS society.

7. Describe how you felt during the challenge using five words and challenge three others to do this through your favorite social media platform.

The challenge will give you a glimpse of the physical restrictions of ALS but nothing except the disease itself can give you a full appreciation of the losses associated with it.

I remember watching people doing the Ice Bucket Challenge in 2014. I had just survived my respiratory arrest and was in the ICU. I did not know the future that was in store for us but I was sure for the first time since being diagnosed with ALS that I wanted to live. I am sure that Pete Frates, Pat Quinn, and Corey Griffin did not know what they were starting at that time. Perhaps my challenge will help their mission to finally make ALS a treatable disease. It only takes one idea and compassionate people to start a movement and make a huge difference.

Let's be still and start moving!

ACKNOWLEDGEMENTS

This project was started during a time of deep grief and I have always believed that I shared a spiritual connection with Zach and Kaya during the writing. I thank them both for helping me move forward with my immense grief and for finally facing the long-locked grief of living with ALS. They are my co-authors and from great tragedy they have manifested a story of resilience, hope and love.

My wife Darlene, whom I love so much, made this book better through her attention to detail. She challenged my vulnerabilities and made sure that each word is true to my beliefs and intentions. Together we have created a book that genuinely represents our state of being, one in which I can take great pride. I am honored to be the father of Zach, Ben, and Nathaniel and proud of the young men they have become—kind and compassionate individuals despite the easier option of withdrawal, bitterness, and anger. They continue to teach me so much and I am grateful to them for seeing me without any limitations.

Along with our family, the Firths—Jennifer, Duncan, Jackson, and Isaac—continue to face the worst situation that families can face, the sudden, inexplicable physical loss of a daughter, and sibling. None of us will ever fully heal from this nor gain an understanding of the 'whys'. I am grateful that our families have been connected through the love of Kaya and Zach.

I am grateful to my mother and father for the loving environment in which I was raised. They gave me a solid foundation that enabled a life of happiness and success. I appreciate their love and support and treasure the memories that we share. I am grateful to Pat and Phyllis for raising their strong and intelligent daughter, Darlene. From the beginning, they welcomed me into their family and took the in-law out of son-in-law. Their unwavering support and love toward us and their grandsons is greatly appreciated.

My brother Brent has always had my back from the time we shared a bedroom to recent years filled with challenges and hardships. He and his family have never stopped caring. I am grateful to Diane, Trevor, and Matty for sacrificing their time with their husband and father to support his regular visits to see me and my family. Brad, Lucia, Alec, Mackenzie and Michaela, I appreciate the countless great memories shared when our families were young.

My cup runs over when it comes to my personal tribe of friends. To my great friends Craig and Carol and our other 'sons', Mackenzie and Hudson, I am grateful that you always go above and beyond to bring our families together and make them whole. I want to thank my friends from early childhood, John (Alisa), Cherrie, Rosalie, Steve (Helen), Andrew (Gail), Alisdair (Elaine), Mike (Sally), Evan (Lenora), Chris and their children, for remaining in my life and keeping me laughing and grounded as we reminisce about our 'merry' years. I am grateful to my medical school friends, Sandy (Farah), Bernie (Johann), Darrell (Kim), Derrick (Wendy), and their children, who despite our geographical distance and my inability to travel have continued to visit me and my family. My local community of friends, Mike and Jennifer, Greg and Judy, Les and Carrie, James and Erin, Mike and Heather, Michael and Mary-Jo, Mike and Jill, Bruce and Shelley, and their children have always felt like extended family and I am grateful for their love and support.

Mary-Jo has chaired our local ALS walk for eight years. I am grateful for her dedication and organizational prowess.

Thanks to Doug and Jaime Matthews and their crew for bringing kindness and laughter into my life and for instilling these attributes in their children. Thanks to Martyn who has treated my family to his amazing kitchen skills since my diagnosis, and who strengthened our friendship at a time when others exited our lives. Thanks to Tim, Terry and Wayne for the new friendships that each brought to my post-diagnosis life. Thanks to Savannah, Erica and Eion for the role they played in the healing of my family. Thanks to Dr. Wei Chu who has selflessly supported me as a friend and family physician from the beginning of this journey. His presence, clinical expertise, and compassion has been of utmost importance during critical times in my life.

A few families have been particularly close to us as we have navigated our adversities. Their tremendous help is acknowledged throughout this book. The Wallace family (James, Erin, Mara, Joe, Sam, and Angie) have been part of our family since Zach and Mara were three months old. During our twenty-five years of friendship, our kids see each other more as siblings than friends. They have supported us through my ALS and felt a profound loss after Zach passed. Tragically, on the same night that I received the advanced copy of this book, my great friend James Douglas Wallace passed suddenly and inexplicably. He was only 53 years-old and in great health. James was one of my dearest friends. He could keep you entertained for hours with his worldly stories and his extensive knowledge about practically everything. He was kind and always generous with his time and talents. I am very grateful for the many fantastic memories we have shared with James, Erin and their wonderful children. I know that James and Zach are working together to help us heal from their physical losses.

Thanks to my spiritual advisors—Reverends Rob Park, Tom Kingston and John McMullin, my parish priests, and Mary-Anne

Kennedy, evidentiary medium—who have reinforced my knowledge that we all belong to something infinitely larger than our physical being.

Working in groups has given my life purpose. Thank you to all of the groups and teams in which I have been involved. In particular, the Georgetown Hospital staff, the Georgetown 'Walk for ALS' committee, ALS Canada, Halton Healthcare Services, The Zach Sutherland and Kaya Firth Resiliency Fund Board of Directors, the Kinsmen Club of Georgetown and the community of Halton Hills.

Thanks to the wonderful women who have worked with me in the office: Marnie, Kelli, Suzanne, Sarah, Nancy, Karen, Sandy, Anna, Marg and Myra. I am grateful for their friendships and support during our many Walks for ALS and our afternoons of meaningful conversation. I am able to live at home due to the care of my nurses, Abraham (Ghattas), Joanne, Yuliya, Sandra and Allison, and my personal care workers, Dorothy, Vanessa and Devinder. They along with numerous caregivers from my past allow me a good night's rest, anticipate my care needs, and tolerate my music selections. Thanks, as well to Daniela for her devotion to my range of motion exercises during the early years of ALS. Her help and that of others has kept me pain free. *Thanks to Dr. Doug McClure and the Georgetown Hospital Respiratory Therapy department for giving me a new airway whenever needed.*

I am grateful for the support of the McMaster ALS Clinic, Dr. John Turnbull, and Dr. Andy Freitag for their help and guidance with my care and the care of others with ALS. Jane Allan holds a special place in my heart. Thanks to Kim, Jamie, and Rob for giving me the power of communication which keeps me happy and productive.

I am humbled by the support of my community and by the generosity of the people who continue to donate to my walk every spring.

I am grateful for the work of my editor and publisher Ken Whyte, my managing editor Matt Bucemi and the team at Sutherland

House. They took a big chance on a new writer and I am grateful for their professionalism and the long nights they spent working a powerful book out of my original manuscript. They have given my eyes a voice, and enabled this legacy for my family.

Finally, I would like to thank all of the patients that I treated over the years. Their trust and support allowed me to make a calling of my job.

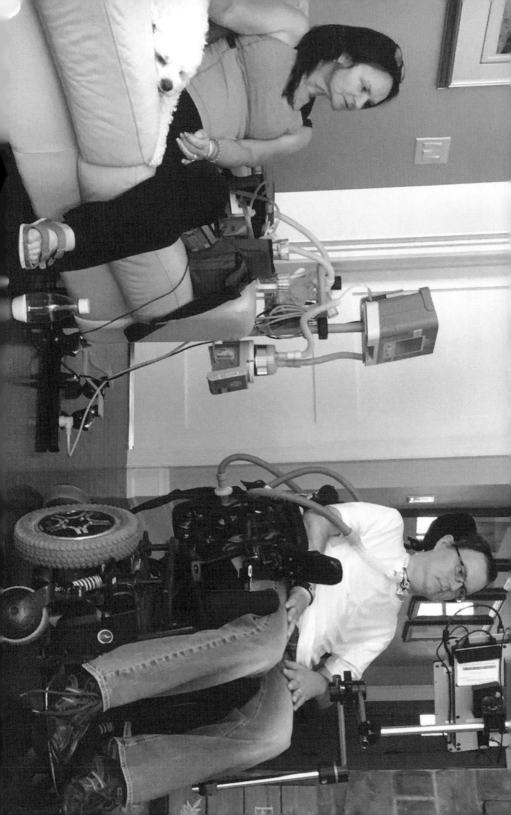